hans kelsen and the case
for democracy

Sandrine Baume

Translated by John Zvesper

First published by the ECPR Press in 2012

Originally published in French under the title *Kelsen: Plaider la démocratie*, © Éditions Michalon 2007. This first English edition, revised and enlarged by the author, © Sandrine Baume 2012

The ECPR Press is the publishing imprint of the European Consortium for Political Research (ECPR), a scholarly association, which supports and encourages the training, research and cross-national cooperation of political scientists in institutions throughout Europe and beyond.

ECPR Press
University of Essex
Wivenhoe Park
Colchester
CO4 3SQ
UK

Typeset by ECPR Press.

Printed and bound by Lightning Source.

British Library Cataloguing-in-Publication Data.

A catalogue record for this book is available from the British Library.

Paperback ISBN: 978-1-907301-24-7

www.ecprnet.eu/ecprpress

Series Editors:
Dario Castiglione (University of Exeter)
Peter Kennealy (European University Institute)
Alexandra Segerberg (Stockholm University)
Peter Triantafillou (Roskilde University)

Publications from the ECPR Press

ECPR Essays:

Just Democracy (ISBN: 9781907301148) Philippe Van Parijs

Is Democracy a Lost Cause? Paradoxes of an Imperfect Invention
(ISBN: 9781907301247) Alfio Mastropaolo

Maestri of Political Science (ISBN: 9781907301193) Donatella Campus,
Gianfranco Pasquino, and Martin Bull

Masters of Political Science (ISBN: 9780955820335) Donatella Campus, and
Gianfranco Pasquino

ECPR Classics:

Beyond the Nation State: (ISBN: 9780955248870) Ernst Haas

*Citizens, Elections, Parties: Approaches to the Comparative Study of the Processes of
Development* (ISBN: 9780955248887) Stein Rokkan

Democracy: Political Finance and state Funding for Parties (ISBN: 9780955248801)
Jack Lively

*Electoral Change: Responses to Evolving Social and Attitudinal Structures in Western
Countries* (ISBN: 9780955820311) Mark Franklin,Thomas Mackie, and Henry Valen

Elite and Specialized Interviewing (ISBN: 9780954796679) Lewis Anthony Dexter

*Identity, Competition and Electoral Availability: The Stabilisation of European
Electorates 1885–1985* (ISBN: 9780955248832) Peter Mair and Stefano Bartolini

Individualism (ISBN: 9780954796662) Steven Lukes

Modern Social Policies in Britain and Sweden: From Relief to Income Maintenance
(ISBN: 9781907301001) Hugh Heclo

Parties and Party Systems: A Framework for Analysis (ISBN: 9780954796617)
Giovanni Sartori

Party Identification and Beyond: Representations of Voting and Party Competition
(ISBN: 9780955820342) Ian Budge, Ivor Crewe, and Dennis Farlie

*People, States and Fear: An Agenda for International Security Studies in the Post-Cold
War Era* (ISBN: 9780955248818) Barry Buzan

Political Elites: (ISBN: 9780954796600) Geraint Parry

Political Theory and Political Science (ISBN: 9781907301025) Martin Landau

State Formation, Parties and Democracy (ISBN: 9781907301179) Hans Daalder

System and Process in International Politics (ISBN: 9780954796624) Morton Kaplan

Territory and Power in the UK: (ISBN: 9780955248863) James Bulpitt

The State Tradition in Western Europe: A Study of an Idea and Institution
(ISBN: 9780955820359) Kenneth Dyson

Please visit www.ecprnet.eu/ecprpress for up-to-date information about new publications.

contents

This book is dedicated to Yannis and to our daughter, Amalia.

acknowledgements

This book could not have been published without the support of Dario Castiglione and Vincent Hoffmann-Martinot, the editors of the ECPR Press. I am also grateful to John Zvesper for his sagacious translation and for the care that he put into this undertaking. The funding for the translation was generously provided by the Foundation Chuard-Schmidt (University of Lausanne). I would like also to thank Ildi Clarke for having so carefully prepared the manuscript. Finally, my deepest gratitude goes to Yannis Papadopoulos, whose support of my writing projects never wavers.

Sandrine Baume
December 2012

It seems, therefore, that a pure theory of law is untimely today, when in great and important countries under the rule of party dictatorships, the most prominent representatives of jurisprudence know no higher task than to serve the political power of the moment.

Hans Kelsen, 'The Function of the Pure Theory of Law', 1937[1]

---

1   Cf. H. Kelsen 'The function of the pure theory of law', in A. Reppy (ed.) *Law: A Century of Progress 1835–1935*, 3 vols., NY: New York University Press and London: OUP, p. 240, 1937.

| preface to the english edition

The few authors who have studied the political thought of Hans Kelsen all agree in the observation that it has never attracted the kind of attention that his theory of law has managed to generate. This does not just apply to non-German-speakers, who might not have access to some of Kelsen's writings because they are not distributed or not translated. The observation holds among German scholars themselves. Kelsen barely emerges as a political thinker. The anecdote recounted by Tamara Ehs in 2009 is very telling here. In 1959, when Roman Schnur proposed to Wilhelm Hennis, his co-editor in the *Politica* series, that they publish a volume dedicated to Hans Kelsen's political thought, Hennis replied that he did not see how such a volume would fit in this series.[1] Half a century later, as Ehs bears out, the case for publishing a book on Kelsen's political thought is still not open-and-shut.[2]

However, observation of the relative obscurity surrounding Kelsen's political thought must be qualified by noticing the repeated efforts to give it some 'visibility.' In this vein, in an article called 'Rechtspositivismus, Demokratie und Gerechtigkeitstheorie' ('Legal Positivism, Democracy and Theory of Justice') (1982),[3] Ota Weinberger was a pioneer or at the very least a booster, in giving to Kelsen's works on democracy and his critique of ideology a status equivalent to that of his theory of law.[4] The 1986 work by Horst Dreier, *Rechtslehre, Staatssoziologie und Demokratietheorie bei Hans Kelsen* (*Theory of Law, Sociology of the State, and Democratic Theory in Hans Kelsen*) was also a decisive step.[5]

---

1 'That you suggested Kelsen was for me incompatible with our tacit agreement, quite apart from the fact that I cannot really imagine what a Kelsen volume would be doing in our series on political science.' Quoted by T. Ehs, 'Vorwort,' in T. Ehs (ed.) *Hans Kelsen: Eine politikwissenschaftliche Einführung*, Baden-Baden: Nomos, 2009, p. 5.

2 ibid. In 1998 Günter Hefler tellingly observed: 'a respectable position within the intellectual sphere was denied to Kelsen. Those who are uninterested in his work on law pay (to this day) no attention to Kelsen.' '*Wissenschaftlichkeit als politischer Einsatz: Methodologie als politische Strategie bei Hans Kelsen und Carl Schmitt*', unpublished diploma thesis, Universität Wien, 1998, pp. 105f., quoted by T. Ehs (ed.) *Hans Kelsen*, p. 6.

3 O. Weinberger, 'Rechtspositivismus, Demokratie und Gerechtigkeitstheorie' in W. Krawietz, E. Toptisch and P. Koller (eds) *Ideologiekritik und demokratietheorie bei Hans Kelsen, Rechtstheorie*, Berlin: Duncker & Humblot, 1982, pp. 501–523.

4 'The scientific significance of Hans Kelsen is in no way restricted to the structural theory of law. His contribution to the theory of democracy and his works on problems in the critique of ideology […] are of equal significance.' O. Weinberger, 'Vorwort,' in W. Krawietz, E. Toptisch and P. Koller (eds) *Ideologiekritik und demokratietheorie*, p. 6.

5 H. Dreier, *Rechtslehre, Staatssoziologie und Demokratietheorie bie Hans Kelsen*, Baden-Baden: Nomos, 1986.

As already indicated above, just as recognition of Kelsen's status as a political thinker was slow in the German-language world, there was a similar tendency in non-German writing, albeit with notable exceptions that we shall come back to. One good indicator of the reception of Kelsen's political theory is the changing tempo in the appearance of translations of *Vom Wesen und Wert der Demokratie* (*Democracy: Its nature and value*) in the West. This text, from 1929, gave a first overview of Kelsen's ideas about democracy, and as such, it occupies a prominent place in his work.[6] The first translations appeared in 1932, in France and Japan. These were soon followed by translations in Czechoslovakia (1933), Spain (1934), Poland (1937) and Turkey (1938). The West's tragic twentieth-century totalitarian experiences – the fascist, Nazi and Bolshevik dictatorships – played a central role in this early (1930s) reception of *Vom Wesen und Wert der Demokratie*. This is very striking in the beautiful preface to the French edition, by Joseph Barthélemy and Boris Mirkine-Guetzévitch:

> At the present hour, of all living jurists, Professor Kelsen emerges as our most distinguished guide in exploring public law doctrines. Especially because democracy is currently being subjected to a general attack from every direction, we should rejoice that the theoretical attack by the proponents of dictatorship is here being answered by an equally theoretical sally, with the most authoritative person in charge of it.[7]

The blossoming of other translations of *Vom Wesen und Wert der Demokratie* had to wait until after the Second World War, with the publication of editions in Italian in 1955, Korean in 1958, Portuguese in 1993, Greek in 1998 and Hebrew in 2005.

One quite surprising thing that emerges from mapping this translation history of *Vom Wesen und Wert der Demokratie* is the absence, right up to the present day, of an English translation.[8] This gap exists in spite of a more than moderate interest

---

6   The first version of *Vom Wesen und Wert der Demokratie*, published in 1920 (Tübingen: J.C.B. Mohr), ran to only 38 pages, much shorter than the 1929 version (by the same publisher), which has 119 pages. In this book (unless otherwise noted), the 1929 version is cited, as published in Hans Kelsen, *Verteidigung der Demokratie*, in M. Jestaedt and O. Lepsius (eds) Tübingen: Mohr Siebeck, 2006, pp. 149–228.

7   J. Barthélemy and B. Mirkine-Guetzévitch, 'Avertissement' (1932), in H. Kelsen, *La Démocratie: sa nature, sa valeur*, French trans. C. Eisenmann, Paris: Dalloz, 2004, p. vi. ('À l'heure présente, et parmi tous les jurisconsultes vivants, le professeur Kelsen apparaît comme le guide le plus illustre dans les investigations doctrinales du droit public. Précisément, la démocratie est actuellement l'objet d'un assaut généralisé partant de toutes les directions. Félicitons-nous de ce que, à l'assaut théorique des partisans de la dictature, il soit répondu par une sortie également théorique, dirigée par l'homme le plus autorisé.')

8   Only a few sections of *Vom Wesen und Wert der Demokratie* have been translated into English: H. Kelsen 'On the Essence and Value of Democracy', in A. J. Jacobson and B. Schlink (eds) *Weimar:*

in political thought and in Kelsen's legal theory, by the English-speaking scientific community. In the case of the United States, the obscurity surrounding Kelsen's work is particularly surprising, given that he spent so much time there – from 1939 to 1973 – and thus, that an important part of his career took place there.[9] It is worth dwelling on the reasons for this obscurity. In 2000, Albert Calsamiglia, perhaps somewhat overstating the point, remarked that even Kelsen's works on legal theory are virtually unknown in North America, barring a few exceptions such as work by Stanley L. Paulson, Ronald Moore, and Michael Hartney.[10]

According to Jeremy Telman, the weak influence of Kelsen in university law departments in America can be explained by their strong resistance to legal positivism, which, as we shall soon see, explains the situation in America not only of Kelsen, but also of a goodly portion of European academic circles. It must also be recalled that Kelsen arrived in the United States at the time when legal realism – a theory competing with positivism – was developing and prospering.[11] In 1962, Karl Llewellyn, a prominent representative of the realist school, judged Kelsen's work to be utterly sterile;[12] that was also Harold Laski's opinion.[13] In the United States, the positivist label claimed by Kelsen was to be one reason for his difficulties in establishing his legal theory, but also for the trouble he was to have in attaining the status of political thinker.[14] As Telman noticed, by trying to separate the science of law from everything pertaining to the extra-legal sphere, especially from politics, Kelsen was swimming against the tide of the view widely held in the United States, summed up in the phrase 'law is politics.'[15]

A jurisprudence of crises, Berkeley, Calif.: University of California Press, 2000, pp. 84–109.

9 See Introduction.

10 A. Calsamiglia, 'For Kelsen', *Ratio Juris*, June 2000, vol. 13, no. 2, p. 199.

11 D. A. J. Telman, 'The Reception of Hans Kelsen's Legal Theory in the United States: A Sociological Model,' January 2008: http://works.bepress.com/jeremy_telman/4, pp. 6–8.

12 'I see Kelsen's work as utterly sterile, save in by-products that derive from his taking his shrewd eyes, for a moment, off what he thinks of as "pure law"'. K. N. Llewellyn, *Jurisprudence: Realism in theory and practice*, Chicago: University of Chicago Press, 1962, p. 356, n. 6, quoted by D. A. J. Telman, 'The Reception of Hans Kelsen's Legal Theory', p. 2, n. 5.

13 Discussing Kelsen's work, Laski, an English political theorist, asserted that it was an 'exercise in logic and not in life.' H. Laski, *A Grammar of Politics*, London: Allen & Unwin, 1938, p. vi.

14 Among the few publications in English that make space for Kelsen's political theory are L. Vinx, *Hans Kelsen's Pure Theory of Law: Legality and legitimacy*, Oxford: Oxford University Press, 2007 (one chapter of which is devoted to Kelsen's democratic theory); and G. De Angelis, 'Ideals and institutions: Hans Kelsen's political theory,' *History of Political Thought*, 2009, vol. 30, no. 3, pp. 524–546.

15 'The very first sentence in the casebook that I used this semester in teaching public international law runs as follows: "First, law is politics." The author of that sentence, Louis Henkin, is one of the editors of the casebook and, as the Chief Reporter for the American Law Institute's Third Restatement of the Foreign Relations Law of the United States, one of the most influential scholars

This low level of interest in Kelsen contrasts with the growing interest of American jurists, and academic circles more generally, in another German-language jurist, and an intellectual enemy of Kelsen: Carl Schmitt. (Richard Posner documents this growing interest in Schmitt.[16]) From this point of view, Schmitt, because his constitutional theory is connected with a substantial political doctrine, is more consonant with the expectations of American jurists. Paradoxically though, this renewed interest in Schmitt's work has sometimes enhanced the 'visibility' of Kelsen's political thought, because thoroughly understanding Schmitt requires knowing the intellectual adversary that he is battling against: Kelsen. Although up to now no book in English has been devoted to Kelsen's political theory, he does appear in studies of the legal-political debates in the Weimar Republic, for example, the work of David Dyzenhaus, *Legality and Legitimacy: Carl Schmitt, Hans Kelsen and Hermann Heller in Weimar* (1999).[17]

While, as previously mentioned, the English-reading public do not have access to a translation of *Vom Wesen und Wert der Democracy*, they do have a text published in English in its first version, in which Kelsen summarises his concept of democracy: a weighty hundred-page article published in 1955 in the journal *Ethics*, entitled 'Foundations of Democracy.'[18] This text is an elaborate theoretical discussion of democracy. Although *Vom Wesen und Wert der Democracy* and 'Foundations of Democracy' are similar conceptually and theoretically, they nevertheless show clear signs of the different contexts from which they emerged. *Vom Wesen und Wert der Demokratie* (1929) was contemporary with the construction of two republics (the German and the Austrian). As a result, institutional considerations loom large in this book, especially those related to the functioning of the parliamentary system and to the issue of representation more generally. 'Foundations of Democracy,' published in the United States in the 1950s, devotes much less space to institutional issues, in order to concentrate on more burning questions about the relationship that there may, or may not, be between political regimes and economic models – or to put it more clearly, between democracy and capitalism. Kelsen reached the conclusion that there is no necessary relationship between them – a conclusion puzzling to some Americans.[19]

---

in the field of public international law.' D. A. J. Telman 'Selective Affinities: On the American Reception of Hans Kelsen's Legal Theory,' Berkeley Electronic Press (bepress) Legal Series Working Paper 1341, May 2006, p. 15: http://law.bepress.com/expresso/eps/1341.

16 Cf. R. A. Posner, *Law, Pragmatism, and Democracy*, Cambridge, Mass.: Harvard University Press, 2003.

17 Oxford, O.U.P.: 1999. See also P. C. Caldwell, *Popular Sovereignty and the Crisis of German Constitutional Law: The theory and practice of Weimar constitutionalism*, Durham and London: Duke University Press, 1997.

18 H. Kelsen, 'Foundations of democracy', *Ethics*, 1955, vol. 66, no. 1, pp. 1–101.

19 Cf. H. Kelsen, 'The function of the pure theory of law', in A. Reppy (ed.) *Law: A Century of Progress 1835–1935*, 3 vols., NY: New York University Press and London: OUP, 1937, p. 94. It should be

One notable feature of Kelsen's reception was that in Italy, much more than in any other country (including other European countries), there were translations of many of his works focussed on political theory. In addition to the translation of *Vom Wesen und Wert der Demokratie* (*Essenza e valore della democrazia,* 1955)[20] there appeared 'Assolutismo e relativismo nella filosofia e nella politica' ('Absolutism and Relativism in Philosophy and Politics') (1955), *I fondamenti della democrazia e altri saggi* (*The Foundations of Democracy and Other Essays*) (1966), *La teoria dello Stato in Dante* (*Dante Alighieri's Theory of the State*) (1974), *Socialismo e stato* (*Socialism and State*) (1978), *La teoria politica del bolscevismo e altri saggi di teoria del diritto e dello Stato* (*The Political Theory of Bolshevism and Other Essays in the Theory of Law and the State*) (1981), *Il primato del parlamento* (*The Primacy of Parliament*) (1982), 'Concezione politica del mondo ed educazione' ('Political World View and Education') (1988), and *Sociologia della democrazia* (*Sociology of Democracy*) (1991).[21] These Italian translations of several of Kelsen's works were followed in the early 1990s by studies of his democratic theory, including those of Agostino Carrino, Gaetano Pecora and Raimondo De Capua.[22] It should be noted that the Italian interest in Kelsen's work is part of the particular attention that has been paid there to the legal-political debate in the German-speaking world during the interwar period, especially to Carl Schmitt but also to Hermann Heller.

In comparison, in France there was quite limited access to Kelsen's political theory. Apart from *Vom Wesen und Wert der Demokratie* (*La Démocratie: sa nature, sa valeur*), really none of his other political theory publications were translated into French.[23] However, since the late 1990s, some studies of Kelsen's political thought have been emerging, with works by Carlos-Miguel Herrera and Sandrine Baume, and the recent collection edited by Olivier Jouanjan.[24] During

---

noted that Kelsen's *General Theory of Law and State*, the first version of which appeared in 1945, also included some reflections on the essential features of democracy, in opposition to autocracy.

20　The first (1920) version of Kelsen's *Vom Wesen und Wert der Demokratie* was translated into Italian during the fascist period, in 1933, in A. Volpicelli (ed.) *Lineamenti di una teoria generale dello stato e altri scritti*, Rome, Anonima Romana Editoriale, pp. 69–99.

21　*Teoria generale del diritto e dello Stato* (*General Theory of Law and State*), which also includes some sections related to the character of democracy, was published in Italian in 1952. For full references of Kelsen's writings mentioned in this chapter see the Select Bibliography of Kelsen's Writings at the end of this book.

22　A. Carrino, *L'ordine delle norme: politica e diritto in Hans Kelsen,* Napoli: Edizioni scientifiche italiane, 1990; G. Pecora, *Il pensiero politico di Kelsen,* Laterza: Bari, 1995; R. De Capua, *Hans Kelsen e il problema della democrazia,* Rome: Carocci, 2003.

23　*General Theory of Law and State* (*Théorie générale du droit et de l'Etat,* published in 1997) could also be mentioned here; cf. notes 19 and 21 in this Preface.

24　C.-M. Herrera, *Théorie juridique et politique chez Hans Kelsen,* Paris: Kimé, 1997; S. Baume, *Kelsen: Plaider la démocratie,* Paris: Michalon, 2007; O. Jouanjan (ed.), *Hans Kelsen: Forme du*

the last ten years, one of the political aspects of Kelsen's works that has generated the most interest in France, has been his thinking about the compatibility between democratic principles and constitutional courts.[25] Thus, *Wer soll der Hüter der Verfassung sein? (Who Should Be the Guardian of the Constitution?)*, published in German in 1931, is one of the most recent of Kelsen's works to be translated into French (*Qui doit être le gardien de la Constitution?* [2006]). It could be argued that in France Kelsen's political works have been used as ammunition in an emotionally-charged debate about constitutional justice.[26]

Hazards in the Reception of Kelsen's Work

Alongside the various circumstances of the reception of Kelsen's work in each particular country, his slow struggle to attain the rank of political thinker remains as a constant that arises from more general factors, which we must try to summarise. His low notoriety as a political thinker stems first of all from misunderstandings and misinterpretations of his thinking. Second, it reflects the difficulties that a significant portion of his audience has had in reconciling the two sides of his work, his theory of democracy and his theory of law – a difficulty so great that some interpreters have seen an internal contradiction here. Third, the reception of Kelsen's political thought was affected by an unfavourable environment. We must look in greater detail at each of these three explanations.

Misunderstandings and Misinterpretations

Among the misunderstandings that surround Kelsen's political thought, two in particular seem to have affected its reception. First is the assumption that his epistemological relativism leads to a kind of amoral or apolitical outlook.[27] As we shall see, Kelsen's relativism actually has strong moral-political implications. It leads both to tolerance and to the promotion of pluralism. His concept of democracy rests on the free flow of ideas; it is coupled with his severe critique of ideology[28] and his defense of minorities.

---

droit et politique de l'autonomie, Paris: PUF, 2010.

25 H. Kelsen, *Qui doit être le gardien de la Constitution?*, Paris: Michel Houdiard, 2006.

26 Cf. O. Beaud *et al.*, *La controverse sur 'le gardien de la Constitution' et la justice constitutionnelle: Kelsen contre Schmitt*, Paris: Panthéon-Assas, 2007.

27 Cf. M. Jestaedt and O. Lepsius, 'Der Rechts- und der Demokratietheoretiker Hans Kelsen – Eine Einführung,' in H. Kelsen, *Verteidigung der Demokratie (Defending Democracy)*, M. Jestaedt and O. Lepsius (eds), Tübingen: Mohr Siebeck, 2006, pp. xv–xvi.

28 O. Weinberger, 'Introduction: Hans Kelsen as philosopher,' in O. Weinberger (ed.) *Hans Kelsen: Essays in legal and moral philosophy*, trans. P. Heath, Dordrecht and Boston: D. Reidel Publishing

Second, the lack of interest generated by Kelsen's political thought also comes from the suspicion that this thought has taken shape somewhere very much tucked away from reality, away from the circumstances of existence. Kelsen is seen as ultimately concerned only with formal questions. In fact, the truth is quite the opposite: Kelsen's political theory is closely geared to observation of the actual functioning of democracies.[29] Moreover, Kelsen spent a lot of time and energy flushing out the myths presented to us by an unrealistic and ideological understanding of democracy, particularly by concepts that homogenise the real, such as the notion of the 'general will.'

Difficulties in Reconciling the Two Sides of Kelsen's Work

If Kelsen's political thought struggles to match in stature his theory of law, this is also because of the difficulties that readers encounter in reconciling the two different sides of his work. How can you harmonise a pure (or positive) theory of law with a democratic theory that ventures into the field of politics, and therefore of values? This question is at the core of the doubts that Kelsen's work inspires, and perhaps explains the relative obscurity of the part of that work – his political thinking – that proves to be tricky, but essential, to reconcile with his theory of law. As we shall see, the centrepiece of this reconciliation consists of Kelsen's epistemological positivism, which secures the coherence of his work. Both his democratic theory and his legal positivism abandon achieving just ruling.[30]

Unfavourable Environment

The limited appeal of Kelsen's political theory also has to do with the particularly unfavourable environment surrounding its reception. His doctrine grew up at a time when legal positivism went into a serious decline, which the twentieth century's two world wars accelerated.[31] This greatly weakened the intellectual position of Kelsen who remained faithful to positivism across the decades. From the Second World War onwards, as Michel Troper emphasises, Kelsen, by rejecting both Marxist and natural right doctrines, marginalised himself with regard to two important terms of political-legal discussion.[32] In this way he was a writer against

---

Company, 1973, pp. xxv – xxvi.

29 See Chapter Two.

30 See Introduction.

31 See Introduction.

32 'Before and during the Second World War, the opponents of fascist dictatorships fought their battles either in the name of an ideal of justice derived from natural right, or in the name of Marxism. In the West, during and after the war, political debate had thus been, and still is, between Marxists

the current, outside the boundaries within which the controversies of the time took place. In the postwar period, Kelsenian positivism was often perceived as providing no consistent response to the dangers – especially from fascists and totalitarians – that brought down several democracies in the twentieth century. Legal-political theory looks for substantial solutions. So Kelsen's view that the very idea of justice is something irrational, and therefore, that justice cannot be an object of knowledge, constituted an important reason for the rejection of his theory. Misunderstanding and disagreement reached their climax with Lon Fuller, an advocate of natural rights, who thought just the opposite: that 'jurisprudence should start with justice.'[33] This assertion led him to neglect and to reject Kelsen's work.

With Kelsen's political theory suspected of being incapable of putting up any substantial resistance to democracy's enemies, its character and its strength have not been appreciated. That strength is found less in a catalogue of intangible values that democracies must adhere to, and more in the conviction that values result from collective decisions, and are therefore contingent. The strength of this position is also its fragility: there are no rational formulas for establishing the values and their contents. Although emotionally our values can seem to us indisputable and supreme, they remain irrational and relative.[34] In 'Foundations of Democracy' Kelsen endorsed the Schumpeterian definition of a civilised man as one who, in contrast to a barbarian, is able to 'realize the relative validity of one's convictions and yet stand for them unflinchingly.'[35] In his view, in democracies the passions that inspire and support political commitments must never obscure the certainty of the relativity of even the most strongly-held convictions.

Kelsen's case for democracy clearly deserves a fuller hearing by political thinkers.

---

and the advocates of the ideology of human rights. Once again, we can see that a doctrine of democracy like Kelsen's, that opposes both camps, arouses little in the way of positive responses.' M. Troper, 'Présentation,' in H. Kelsen, *La Démocratie: sa nature, sa valeur* (C. Eisenmann's 1932 translation of *Vom Wesen und Wert der Demokratie*), Paris: Economica, 1988, p. 11.

33 'I share the opinion of Jerome Hall, evidenced in his excellent *Readings*, that jurisprudence should start with justice. I place this preference not on exhortatory grounds, but on a belief that until one has wrestled with the problem of justice one cannot truly understand the other issues of jurisprudence. Kelsen, for example, excludes justice from his studies because it is an 'irrational ideal' and therefore 'not subject to cognition.' The whole structure of his theory derives from that exclusion. The meaning of his theory can therefore be understood only when we have subjected to critical scrutiny its keystone of negation.' L. Fuller, 'The place and uses of jurisprudence in the law school curriculum,' *Journal of Legal Education*, 1948–1949, 1, p. 496.

34 Cf. H. Kelsen, 'Foundations of democracy', p. 4.

35 'To realize the relative validity of one's convictions and yet stand for them unflinchingly is what distinguishes a civilized man from a barbarian.' Cf. ibid. Kelsen here refers to J. A. Schumpeter, *Capitalism, Socialism and Democracy*, New York and London: Harper & Bros, 1942, p. 242.

introduction

At the end of the First World War, Austria and Germany tried out a democratic political system, hastily built upon the ruins of their empire. During the 1920s the innovations that the Republic embodied, and the fears that it inspired, gave rise to some intense debate, to which Hans Kelsen made a major contribution. In response to antiparliamentary arguments and to a kind of disenchantment with political institutions, he offered a definition of democracy that met the standard, and often-repeated objections to it. The political upheavals that emerged in 1918 stirred up the question of the stability of democratic institutions, an issue that became central not only for Kelsen but also for other jurists, such as Carl Schmitt (1888–1985), Hermann Heller (1891–1933), Rudolf Smend (1881–1975), and Erich Kaufmann (1880–1972). We should not let the variety of their reactions resulting from their diverging doctrinal positions – liberal, social-democratic, statist or even authoritarian – obscure the fact that they all shared a constant concern with a bundle of basic questions about the sustainability of the state and how a social plurality can coexist politically. That these discussions emerged in a post-imperial context, in which democracy had been in place only a few years, added intensity and perhaps also a degree of clarity to these questions that urgently demanded answers.

In the widely-known work of Kelsen, the theory of democracy is not tangential; it is intimately tied to his thinking about law, primarily in his refusal to surrender to any of the mythologies that denature the investigation of legal and political phenomena. His legal positivism and his reflections on the characteristics of democracy echo each other, and set out a coherent doctrine profoundly marked by relativism. In the first place, Kelsen's understanding of democracy has rid itself of the fictions of the 'general will', of political oneness, and of the objective interest of the state; the Kelsenian understanding takes conflicts of interest to be the central objects of enquiry, and resolutions of these conflicts occur only through compromises. In the second place, his definition of law, that of legal positivism, renounces all claims to produce just ruling.

While Hans Kelsen has left his mark on the twentieth century with his prolific work, his biography and his intellectual trajectory are interwoven with the tragic events of that century; in fact, in a way, what he wrote was a commentary on that century.

Kelsen was born into a family of Jewish origin in Prague on October 11th, 1881.[1] In 1884 the family moved to Vienna and it was here that Kelsen committed

---

1 Much valuable biographical information has been supplied by the recent republication of the 1947 autobiography of Kelsen, in *Hans Kelsen im Selbstzeugnis*, M. Jestaedt (ed.), Tübingen: Mohr Siebeck, 2006, and by R. A. Métall's biography, *Hans Kelsen: Leben und Werk*, Wien: F. Deuticke, 1969.

himself to the study of law, even though his first choices had been in the direction of philosophy, mathematics and physics. He obtained his doctorate in 1906. During his formative years his work focused especially on the history of ideas, and he published a notable book in this field, *Die Staatslehre des Dante Alighieri* (*Dante Alighieri's Theory of the State*) (1905).[2] Thanks to a substantial grant, he spent a period, starting in 1908, at the University of Heidelberg, where he attended the seminars of Georg Jellinek (1851–1911), who was then considered to be an authority on the theory of the state ('allgemeine Staatslehre'). The young Kelsen was disappointed with these seminars, as he was with the personality of the professor, who was vain and not one for intellectual controversy.[3] The time that Kelsen spent in Heidelberg enabled him to do a rough draft of his habilitation thesis, which when published in 1911, he called *Hauptprobleme des Staatsrechtslehre* (*Principal Problems in the Theory of Public Law*). It was in this voluminous publication that his pure theory of law took shape. In autumn 1911 Kelsen was named privat-dozent at the University of Vienna, where he taught public law and the philosophy of law. This appointment opened up to him an academic career that his religious background would never facilitate. In 1914, together with Edmund Bernatzik, Adolf Menzel, Henrich Lammasch and Max Hussarek, he founded the *Austrian Journal of Public Law* (*Öffentliches Recht für Österreichischen Zetischrift*).[4] Three years later he became extraordinary professor, then, in 1919, he succeeded Edmund Bernatzik (1854–1919) in the position of professor in public and administrative law.

During the First World War and continuing right on up to the end of the monarchy, Kelsen was drafted into the legal department of the War Ministry. He published little during these troubled times, but his scientific activity never stopped. In fact it was during this period that he reworked the concept of sovereignty, resulting in his essay *Das Problem der Souveränität und die Theorie des Völkerrechts; Beitrag zu einer reinen Rechtslehre (The Problem of Sovereignty and the Theory of International Law: A contribution to a pure theory of law)* (1920). Moreover, Kelsen gathered around him in private seminars some of his students, including Adolf Merkl, Alfred Verdross, and Eric Voegelin (at that time written Erich Vögelin). In these seminar meetings was born the Vienna School. In October 1918, when Kelsen had resumed all his academic activities, Karl Renner, the Chancellor in Austria's provisional government, assigned to him the task of writing the final draft of the Constitution, which Chancellor Renner believed must respect both the principle of federalism and that of democracy, while remaining compatible with a system

---

2   Bibliographic details of Kelsen's work listed in this chapter can be found, in order of the date of original publication, in the Select Bibliography of Kelsen's Writings at the end of the book.

3   This assessment is clear in his autobiography, where he says of Jellinek: 'He could not bear the slightest contradiction, which I noticed too late so I probably forfeited his favour', *Hans Kelsen im Selbstzeugnis*, p. 41.

4   Kelsen's Jewish origins meant that in 1934 he was compelled to leave the editorial committee.

of political representation. In doing this work, Kelsen paid particular attention to crafting a constitutional court, an institution that is often linked with his name.

During the 1920s Kelsen extended his works in legal and political theory, which permeate each other. This period is full of intense scientific activity and a large number of publications. At the same time, he continued his university teaching and acted as a judge on Austria's Constitutional Court, to which he was to be appointed for life. During his years as a professor in Austria, Kelsen remained ideologically close to the Social Democratic Party (SDP), without officially joining it. His independence from political parties always seemed to him to be essential for conducting his professional duties.[5] During the 1920s the political climate became more hostile to him: the growing influence of the Christian Social Party (CSP) upset the balance that still favoured the SDP after the adoption of the Constitution. Kelsen thus began to experience a period of personal and professional insecurity. Starting in 1929, the Austrian Constitutional Court, with which he was identified, was targeted with virulent attacks by the CSP, aimed especially at the Court's decisions related to matrimonial waivers ('Dispensehen'). On this issue, Kelsen adopted the secular position and rejected the Catholic principle of the indissolubility of marriage. Therefore, as a Constitutional judge, he refused to invalidate, by court order, the marriage of a Catholic couple in which one partner's first marriage had been dissolved by an administrative body. Austrian civil law contained two conflicting principles: on the one hand the indissolubility of marriage and on the other, the unlimited jurisdiction of the civil administration to grant a 'matrimonial waiver' that allowed separated spouses, including Catholics, to remarry. In response to Catholic pressure, the CSP press launched a slanderous campaign against the Constitutional Court. Having played a significant part in this decision, Kelsen was targeted by sometimes downright filthy attacks, which went as far as accusing him of promoting bigamy.[6] These events, together with reforms of the judicial appointment process, hastened the end of his work on the Constitutional Court, his decision to leave Austria, and his departure to the University of Cologne in 1930, the first of his many migrations.

Kelsen found no lasting tranquillity in Germany; his situation was soon threatened again. Hitler's accession to the Chancellery at the end of January 1933 confirmed Kelsen's belief that his days in Cologne were henceforth numbered. He was among the first of the professors laid off by the Nazi regime in pursuance of their law of April 7th, 1933, called the 'Law for the Restoration of the Professional

---

5   'My need for independence from partisan politics, in my profession, was and is stronger than this sympathy. What I do not allow to the state – restriction on the right and freedom of research and expression of opinions – I cannot concede to a political party by voluntary submission to their discipline'. From Hans Kelsen's autobiography, quoted in Métall, *Hans Kelsen: Leben und Werk*, p. 33.

6   Kelsen went over these events in some detail in his autobiography; cf. *Hans Kelsen im Selbstzeugnis*, pp. 72–79.

Civil Service' (*Gesetz zur Wiederherstellung des Berufsbeamtentums*). In the spring of 1933, Kelsen fled Germany with his wife and their two daughters. In autumn that year he moved to Geneva, where he received, from William Rappard, an invitation to the University Institute of Advanced International Studies.[7] It was in this period that he published the first version of his *Pure Theory of Law*, but this did not mean that he stopped reflecting on politics, as can be seen especially from the publication in 1934 of *La Dictature de Parti* ('The Party Dictatorship'). In autumn 1936 Kelsen was appointed to a post at the German University of Prague, but he was immediately subjected to pressure from students with '*völkisch*' allegiance, which weakened his position and placed impossible pressures on him. In 1938 he stopped teaching there and returned to Geneva, where his wife lived. When war broke out in September 1939, Kelsen, firmly convinced that Switzerland could not escape invasion and preserve its neutrality, accepted the necessity of leaving Europe. So at 59 years of age, he set off for the United States, where starting in 1940, he taught at Harvard University and then from 1942, at the University of California, Berkeley. Although he then dedicated a significant part of his publications to international law (*The Law of the United Nations* (1950), *Principles of International Law* (1952), *Collective Security under International Law* (1954)), he did not abandon his work on theories of the state and of democracy (*General Theory of Law and State* (1945), 'Foundations of Democracy' (1955)). Caught up in the tragic history of the tumultuous twentieth century, after the end of the Second World War Kelsen was legal advisor to the United Nations War Crimes Commission in Washington, and was responsible for preparing the legal aspects of the Nuremberg Trials. His farewell lecture at UC Berkeley in May 1952 marked the beginning of his university retirement. During the last twenty years of his life there was a degree of intellectual recognition of his work, especially its legal aspects. Several honorary doctorates were bestowed on him, notably by UC Berkeley (1952), the Universidad Nacional Autónoma de México (1960), the Freie Universität Berlin (1961), the Universität Wien (1961), the New School for Social Research (1961), and by the Universities of Paris (1963), Salzburg (1967) and Strasbourg (1972).[8] On April 19th, 1973, in his 92nd year, Hans Kelsen died in Berkeley, leaving a body of work that had come through the vicissitudes of his life without losing any of its intellectual force.

---

7   In 1933 Kelsen received offers to pursue his academic career outside Germany and Austria from three different institutions: the London School of Economics and Political Science, the New School for Social Research in New York, and the University Institute of Advanced International Studies (*l'Institut Universitaire des Hautes Etudes Internationales*) in Geneva. His language skills being much better in French than in English, he opted for Geneva.

8   In 1936 Kelsen had already received two honorary doctorates, from Harvard University and from the Rijksuniversiteit Utrecht. This information is provided by the timeline constructed by M. Jestaedt in *Hans Kelsen im Selbstzeugnis*, (1947) in Jestaedt (ed.) 2006, pp. 97–105.

This sketch of Kelsen's personal history does not do justice to the richness of his intellectual biography, and it gives only a very approximate idea of the tenor of his work. When he was 46, he sent an autobiographical letter to a Hungarian professor, Julius Moor (1888–1950),[9] in which he looked back over the main lines of his research. Kelsen's missive contains very few of the striking events of his life: no trace of the First World War, the end of the Empire, or his first years as a professor. All the space is occupied instead by the unfolding of his research work and its underlying intellectual questions. At the summit of the first insights that Kelsen arrived at, and that decisively directed his intellectual trajectory, was the idea that law is by nature normative. This assertion was not at all obvious, as is clear from the numerous challenges that it was to be subjected to. Kelsen also asserted that legal theory should consist exclusively of the study of norms and should not be mixed up with sociological or political considerations. His pure theory of law is primarily a struggle against methodological syncretism. In *Über Grenzen zwischen juristischer und soziologischer Methode* (*On the Borders between Legal and Sociological Method*) (1911), he strongly emphasises the incompatibility of sociology and legal science, of is and ought, of causal and normative.[10] In 1927 he recognised his debt to Kantianism on this methodological point that determines much of his pure theory of law:

> Purity of method, indispensable to legal science, did not seem to me to be guaranteed by any philosopher as sharply as by Kant with his contrast between Is and Ought. Thus for me, Kantian philosophy was from the very outset the light that guided me.[11]

Kelsen denounces the ever-tempting confusion between legal theory and 'political trends', whether or not these trends are conscious.

Kelsen's discovery that examination of the legal sphere must be strictly normative is complemented by a second basic idea, that the state falls exclusively within the realm of the ought, that it is first and foremost a coercive command that applies the law. For Kelsen, there follows from this an identity between the laws and the state. This assumed unity between these two spheres incited very lively disapproval, especially among the jurists Erich Kaufmann, Hermann Heller, Carl Schmitt, and Rudolf Smend, who saw in it a harmful reduction of the state to the simple execution of laws, leaving no room for the expression of the special functions of the state. This disapproval extended beyond Germany, especially to certain French constitutionalists such as Léon Duguit (1859–1928) who feared

---

9 H. Kelsen, 'Selbstdarstellung' (1927) in Jestaedt (ed.), *Hans Kelsen im Selbstzeugnis*, pp. 21–29. Julius (Gyula) Moor is considered to have been the preeminent Hungarian philosopher of law.

10 H. Kelsen, *Über Grenzen zwischen juristischer und soziologischer Methode*, Tübingen: J.C.B. Mohr, 1911, especially pp. 10–11.

11 H. Kelsen, 'Selbstdarstellung' (1927), p. 23.

that 'if we identify the state and the law as Kelsen does, it seems very difficult for the law to set any limitation on the state'.[12] In a paradox that is merely apparent, the identity of law and state, which Kelsen sets forth as an essential linchpin of his scientific work, has strong political implications. The state secures its unity only by the submission of its members to a common legal order, never by any kind of sociological chemistry.[13] This idea shatters all attempts to establish the unity of the state on components that are national, religious, ethnic, and so on. Moreover, the state can never claim independence from the law. The sphere of the state has no supra-juridic existence; it must never become autonomous from the law. The state is merely the body that executes the law; it has no 'transcendent' origin.

In his autobiographical letter, Kelsen mixes into his legal considerations some very illuminating specifics about his political theory. He emphasises the relationship, which he never denied, between democracy and a form of relativism and empiricism. Or, differently expressed, an essential link between autocracy and a metaphysical and absolute conception of the world. That was a relationship that had already appeared in a text published in 1913 ('Politische Weltanschauung und Erziehung' ('Political World View and Education')), and that ran through all of Kelsen's political thought.

---

12 C.-M. Herrera, *Théorie juridique et politique chez Hans Kelsen*, Paris: Kimé, 1997, p. 17.
13 See Chapter Three, Section 1: 'The Legal Order as the Ultimate Source of Cohesion'.

chapter one | rules without transcendence

The Significance of Legal Positivism

By removing from law all extralegal ingredients, Hans Kelsen adopts the tenets of legal positivism. These had been developed in the second half of the nineteenth century, especially in the theories of Paul Laband (1838–1918) and Carl Friedrich von Gerber (1823–1891), which were elaborated and radicalised by Kelsen's work. In broad outline, the intellectual project of positivism consists of this attempt to have a science of law with no non-legal elements – i.e. no ethics or politics. 'Law has no foundation other than law itself': for Norberto Bobbio, that expresses the quintessence of legal positivism. Likewise, the foundation of law consists in the validity of legal norms.[1] What distinguishes positivism from antipositivist doctrines, such as natural law, is the idea that law is a product of the will and of human authority, and does not refer to a system of thought, norms or values that transcends it. When, in 1928, Kelsen contrasted positivism with natural law, he stated:

> This is where the 'positivity' of a legal system comes in, as compared with the law of nature: it is made ['posed'] by human will – a ground of validity thoroughly alien to natural law because, as a 'natural' order, it is not created by man and by its own assumption cannot be created by a human act. In this lies the contrast between a material and a formal principle of validity.[2]

---

1   'Positivism is not concerned with the axiological justification of norms, with the foundation understood as a problem of the value of the norms. *Jus quia iussum non quia iustum.* So it becomes perfectly natural, and perfectly compatible with the logic of the system, for a norm be considered valid provided it is imposed by an authority that has received the power to issue binding norms, which in turn has received that power from an even higher authority, and so on. Since for a positivist the problem of the foundation of law comes down to the problem of its validity, the assertion that the foundation of law is law itself, becomes legitimate and understandable: validity is simply a legal status, unlike value, which presupposes the presence of ethical assumptions or of considerations of political expediency.' N. Bobbio, *Essais sur la théorie du droit*, Paris: Bruylant, LGDJ, 1998, p. 235.

2   H. Kelsen, *General Theory of Law and State*, trans. A. Wedberg, Cambridge, Mass.: Harvard University Press, 1945, p. 392. (Reprinted in Clark, New Jersey by The Lawbook Exchange, Ltd., 2011).

The norms of natural law are not valid because they are posed by human authority, but only because 'they stem from God, nature or reason and thus are good, right and just'.[3]

In contrast, for the positivist, law must not be revealed, it must be created as a product of a human action, a decision rather than a cognitive process. And it is here that the battle will be joined. Resistance to legal positivism consists for a significant part in its liberation from external justifications (i.e. ethical, political, or religious) in the legal sphere, and in its renunciation of knowing what constitutes just and true ruling. In 1945, in his *General Theory of Law and State*, Kelsen explicitly linked legal positivism with relativism, and in fact coupled natural law with metaphysical absolutism:

> Any attempt to push beyond the relative-hypothetical foundations of positive law, that is, to move from a hypothetical to an absolutely valid fundamental norm justifying the validity of positive law (an attempt which for obvious political reasons recurs often enough), means the abandonment of the distinction between positive and natural law. It means the invasion of natural-law theory into the scientific treatment of positive law, and, if an analogy with the natural sciences is permissible, an intrusion of metaphysics into the realm of science.[4]

The Kelsenian demand for independence from all political persuasions coincides with a desire to endow the science of law with objectivity and ultimately, a scientific character. This is the agenda of the pure theory of law.[5] Accepting the assumptions of legal positivism means renouncing the claim to produce just solutions to social conflicts. In an article that he published in 1936, two years after the publication of his *Pure Theory of Law,* Kelsen listed some objections that were challenging legal positivism from various quarters. The distance that legal positivism maintained from the political sphere had opened the door to two criticisms: on the one hand, that by separating itself from reality it loses all scientific value, and on the other hand that it fails to respect its own premises, by (unavowedly) serving a rather diverse number of political interests. To the first objection, Kelsen retorted that it is precisely by its freedom from political values that positivist doctrines acquire their scientific quality.[6] As for the second criticism, Kelsen disputes it by

---

3   ibid.

4   ibid., p. 396.

5   'Jurisprudence had been almost completely reduced – openly or covertly – to deliberations of legal policy, and my aim from the very beginning was to raise it to the level of a genuine science, a human science.' Preface to the first edition of H. Kelsen, *Reine Rechtslehre* (1934) (Pure Theory of Law), translated into English as *Introduction to the Problems of Legal Theory*, trans. B. Litschewski Paulson and S. L. Paulson, Introduction by S. L. Paulson, Oxford: Clarendon Press, 1992.

6   This idea was very well expressed by Norberto Bobbio: 'In Kelsen too, the intention of bringing the science of law up to the level of the other sciences by pursuing the ideal of objectivity and

showing the contradictory nature of such objections when formulated against the pure theory of law:

> Fascists see in it a democratic liberalism; democrats regard it as a pacemaker of fascism. Communists disqualify it as the ideology of a capitalistic etatism; nationalists and capitalists either as pure bolshevism or as concealed anarchism. Some say that its spirit is related to the Catholic thinking of scholastic philosophy, whereas others believe they see in it the characteristic criteria of a Protestant jurisprudence. And there are others who would like to stigmatise it as being atheistic. In a word, there is no political movement which the pure theory of law has not yet been suspected of favouring. But nothing could prove better its *purity*.[7]

According to Kelsen, a norm that is just ('*gerecht*') is so only in a relative way, not by its conformity to a positive norm. If 'absolute' values, such as justice or equity, exist, they do not fall within the ambit of the science of law, and thus they cannot be defined by it. For Kelsen, the evolution of the definition of justice and its successive shifts in meaning, constitute the demonstration that it cannot be an object of rational knowledge. This is a view that was not to be shared by John Rawls, for whom objective reasoning and rational procedures of deliberation can define the principles of justice.[8] In contrast, Kelsen remained very sceptical about all rational attempts to choose values and to define their content. Therefore justice as a value is not within the ken of the science of law:

> For justice, generally considered as an order distinct from and superior to positive law, is in its absolute value beyond experience, just as the Platonic idea is beyond reality, or the thing in itself transcends the phenomena. The dualism of justice and positive law is just as metaphysical as this ontological dualism. And like the latter dualism, the former equally serves a dual purpose, depending on the spirit in which it is invoked: optimistic and conservative, or pessimistic and revolutionary. It can be used either to justify the given as a natural or social order because it conforms to an ideal, or to deny and to reject it because of its non-conformity.[9]

---

accuracy, goes with an irrationalist conception of values that is quite as radical as it is in Pareto and Weber. Scientists who want to succeed in their intention to build a universally valid theory must as much as possible shy away from value judgements, precisely because values represent the sphere of the irrational.' *Essais sur la théorie du droit*, p. 213.

7   H. Kelsen, 'The Function of the Pure Theory of Law,' (1936), in A. Reppy (ed.), *Law: A Century of Progress 1835–1935*, vol. 2., New York: New York University Press and London: Oxford University Press, 1937, p. 239.

8   For a critique of the formation of values in John Rawls, cf. R. Boudon, *Le Juste et le vrai: Études sur l'objectivité des valeurs et de la connaissance*, Paris: Fayard, 1995, especially pp. 49 and 371.

9   H. Kelsen, 'La Méthode et la notion fondamentale de la théorie pure du droit', *Revue de*

In Kelsen's understanding of law, as in his democratic theory for that matter, absolute values cannot be included without being subordinate to an ideology that necessarily has 'its roots in the will, in desire, not in knowledge' but in interests.[10] Values are fragile standards that constitute a 'metaphysical' source of legitimacy that Kelsen cannot come to terms with. So with great consistency, he turns to legality as the ultimate criterion for legitimacy. The equivalence between legitimacy and legality that he sets up, especially in *Allgemeine Staatslehre* (1925) (*General Theory of the State*), follows from his pure theory of law, the intention of which is to exclude from legal science, all political, metaphysical and moral considerations – in fact all fields that are foreign to the subject of law. So the legitimacy of a norm is limited to its legality or its validity. This is a hallmark of the positivist program:

> The validity of legal norms may be limited in time, and it is important to notice that the end as well as the beginning of this validity is determined only by the order to which they belong. They remain valid as long as they have not been invalidated in the way which the legal order itself determines. This is the principle of legitimacy.[11]

In a virulent critique of the Kelsenian equation of legitimacy with legality, Carl Schmitt favoured legitimacy over legality, the political over the legal. He contrasted the 'mystification' of logico-legalistic procedures with the irrefragability of political decisions. In Kelsen's equation of legality and legitimacy, of the law and the state, Schmitt saw an eclipse of decisions, including those that are required in exceptional cases and that are, for Schmitt, the very essence of the political. Schmitt's objections were the most vehement reaction against Kelsenian 'formalism'. Their arguments derived from the dysfunctioning of the Weimar Republic, especially the fragility and instability of its parliamentary system. Strict adherence to legality did nothing to ensure political unity and stability, which according to Schmitt, depended on the legitimacy of the sovereign, i.e. the legitimacy of the President of the Reich. In contrast to Schmitt, and with great confidence in parliamentary mechanisms, Kelsen did not contemplate demands dealing with situations of state emergencies calling for extra-legal responses.

The battle that Kelsen led for the independence of the science of law from political persuasions, took place in a period when Europe lived and suffered through new forms of autocracy: the fascist, Nazi and Bolshevik dictatorships. This call for independence was clearly a condemnation of those jurists who, in 'the current pestiferous atmosphere',[12] placed their knowledge at the disposal of

---

Métaphysique et de Morale, 1934, p. 189.

10 ibid., p. 191.

11 H. Kelsen, *General Theory of Law and State*, p. 117.

12 Kelsen used this expression in August 1933 in a letter addressed to Renato Treves, published in the journal *Droit & Société*, 1987, no. 7, p. 327.

the political power of the moment.[13] This is an aspect of positivism that has been insufficiently noticed by those intellectuals who have reproached it for placing itself in the service of the Prince. Antipositivist criticism directed at Kelsen was expressed even before the postwar period. When in 1925 Kelsen published *Allgemeine Staatslehre* – which was a positivist manifesto – he was taking a stance against the first period in which German positivism was in decline. From 1870 to 1914[14] positivism had been virtually unchallenged. But after the First World War, especially among jurists, there emerged a doctrinal opposition that restored sociological, moral and political considerations in the theory of law and the state, against the positivist methodological program that was trying to liberate law from any extralegal component. As Kelsen perfectly understood,[15] the First World War played an important role in the rejection of positivism, and the Second World War discredited positivists even more.[16] In the 1920s and 1930s there were still many proponents of positivism, such as Kelsen, Anschütz, Thoma, Rothenbücher, Stier-Somlo, Giese, and Nawiasky; after the Second World War, antipositivists, among them Smend, Kaufmann, Leibholz, and Scheuner, came to occupy most of the terrain.[17] A good illustration of this return after 1945 to the doctrines of natural law, to foundational values, and to certain metaphysical beliefs, is an article published in 1967 by Alexandre Passerin d'Entrèves (1902–1985), 'Légalité et légitimité' ('Legality and Legitimacy').[18] According to Passerin d'Entrèves,

> the principle of legality no longer merely requires that the rules and decisions that comprise the system be formally correct. It also requires that they be congruent with certain values, the values that are described as necessary for 'the existence of a free society'. These values are the touchstone of the law, and the substantive side of legality.[19]

---

13 Cf. the epigraph of this book.

14 Cf. P. von Oertzen, *Die soziale Funktion des staatsrecthlichen Positivismus: eine wissensoziologische Studie über die Entstehung des formalistischen Positivismus in der deutschen Staatsrechtswissenschaft*, Frankfurt am Main: Suhrkamp Verlag, 1974, p. 8.

15 'Since the social turmoil brought about by the World War, the traditional theory of law has been going right back to the doctrine of natural law, just as traditional philosophy has been returning to pre-Kantian metaphysics. Finding itself in the same situation as the feudal nobility at the beginning of the nineteenth century, the bourgeoisie of the twentieth century is resorting to exactly the same political ideologies that that nobility had championed against the bourgeoisie.' H. Kelsen, 'La Méthode et la notion'..., p. 195.

16 M. Stolleis, *Der Methodenstreit der Weimarer Staatsrechtslehre – ein abgeschlossenes Kapitel der Wissenschaftsgeschichte?*, Stuttgart: Franz Steiner, 2001, p. 19.

17 ibid.

18 Passerin d'Entrèves notes in this article (in P. Bastid *et al.*, *L'idée de légitimité*, Paris: PUF, 1967, p. 29) that it was inspired by the title of Schmitt's essay of 1932, 'Legalität und Legitimität'.

19 ibid, p. 39.

To resort to the 'cult of legality' in order to resolve ideological differences and the multiplicity of values, so fully experienced in the twentieth century, amounts 'to muting the underlying problems'.[20] If respecting the principles of the rule of law, such as popular sovereignty, can produce systems that are legal but unjust, then that demonstrates that legality does not tally with legitimacy.

After the Second World War, the Kelsenian refusal to include consideration of values in legal theory has sometimes been regarded as leaving the door open to oppressive regimes, which the twentieth century sadly saw so much of. But before too hastily condemning Kelsen's pure theory of law, we must recognise its liberating purpose, which consisted of never making legal theory an ally of any political interest whatsoever: 'In particular it [the pure theory of law] refuses to serve any political interests whatsoever, by refusing to furnish them with the ideologies needed to justify or to discredit the existing social order'.[21]

In 1955, in 'Foundations of Democracy', Kelsen discusses the criticism of Christian thinkers, such as the protestant theologians Emil Brunner and Reinhold Niebuhr, according to whom positivist relativism bears some responsibility for the development of twentieth-century totalitarianisms, because of its failure to oppose them intellectually. These thinkers accused positivist doctrines of having weakened the concept of justice by relativising it;[22] by giving up on the idea of absolute and divine justice, positivism prepared the ground for totalitarianism.[23] For Kelsen, this relationship between positivism and totalitarianism is invalidated by reading the texts, which shows that the traditional justifications of totalitarianism have been supplied more by antirelativist than by relativist philosophy. In this connection he mentions the philosophic absolutism of Plato.[24]

---

20 ibid, p. 35.

21 H. Kelsen, 'La Méthode et la notion...', p. 191.

22 Kelsen here takes up some arguments made by detractors of positivist doctrines: 'It was, however, the positivism of the nineteenth century, with its denial of the metaphysical and superhuman, which dissolved the idea of justice by proclaiming the relativity of all views of justice. Thereby the idea of justice was stripped of all divine dignity and law abandoned to the vagaries of human will. The view that justice is of its nature relative became the dogma of the jurists.' E. Brunner, *Gerechtigkeit: Eine Lehre von den Grundgesetzen der Gesellschaftsordnung*, Zürich: Zwingli Verlag, 1943, quoted by Kelsen ('Foundations of democracy', *Ethics*, 1955, vol. 66, no. 1, p. 41) from the English translation by M. Hottinger, *Justice and the Social Order*, London and Redhill: Lutterworth Press, New York: Harper & Bros, 1945, p. 15.

23 'The totalitarian state, this "monster of injustice", is not "the invention of a handful of criminals in the grand style", but "the ineluctable consequence" of a "positivism void of faith and inimical to metaphysics and religion", "the inevitable result of man's loss of faith in a *divine* law, in an eternal justice"'. E. Brunner, *Justice and the Social Order*, pp. 16–17, is here being quoted by Kelsen, in 'Foundations of democracy', p. 42.

24 'Besides, Brunner's assertion that relativism is responsible for the totalitarian state is in open contradiction to the undeniable fact that the classical justification of the totalitarian state, as

The Relativistic Foundations of Democracy

The consistency between Kelsen's theory of law and his political theory follows especially from his relativism, which went along with a value irrationalism. In accordance with his positivist doctrine, legal norms can be assessed only in terms of their legality, not with reference to absolute values. Similarly, Kelsen refused to relate democratic theory to intangible values. He did not define democracy substantially; he did not recognise a 'good' that democratic regimes should aim at. A democratic system necessarily implies a critical, relativistic perspective. That is one possible criterion for distinguishing autocracy from democracy: whilst the former is weighed down with absolute values or an incontestable definition of the good, the latter puts values into a discursive competition, the results of which are uncertain. In democratic regimes there is no possibility of establishing political programs based on truth. Every proposal competes with divergent political views. Moreover, in theory each and every conviction has the same chance of winning this competition and thereby becoming the new majority view.[25] This essential relationship that Kelsen sets up between democracy and relativism is also the key to understanding his view of the parliamentary process: neither the majority nor the minority can claim to have the truth, they can only try to persuade, which for the majority means trying to persist, and for the minority means trying to overturn the balance of power. For this reason, in a parliamentary democracy neither the majority nor the minority can ignore the opposing viewpoint; in fact, they must constantly consider it. It is not the best opinion but the opinion of the majority that rules, and this gives majority opinion a relative status.

This 'primitive' association that Kelsen makes between democracy and relativism was perfectly understood by his radical intellectual enemy, Carl Schmitt:

> When Kelsen gives the reasons for opting for democracy, he openly reveals the mathematical and natural-scientific character of his thinking. Democracy is the expression of a political relativism and a scientific orientation that are *liberated from miracles* and dogmas and based on human understanding and critical doubt.[26]

pointed out earlier, is furnished just by that philosophy which more than any other has rejected relativism and emphatically asserted the transcendental existence of absolute values – Plato's doctrine of the ideas on the basis of which he outlined the constitution of his ideal state, which in every respect is a totalitarian autocracy. Totalitarian ideologists, therefore, have always referred to Plato's philosophical absolutism and recognized in the Platonic state the model for their political schemes.' H. Kelsen, 'Foundations of democracy', pp. 42–43.

25 Cf. H. Kelsen, 'State-form and world-outlook', [1933] in O. Weinberger (ed. and intro.), *Hans Kelsen: Essays in Legal and Moral Philosophy*, trans. P. Heath, Dordrecht (Netherlands) and Boston (USA): D. Reidel Publishing Company, 1973, pp. 111–112.

26 C. Schmitt, *Political Theology: Four Chapters on the Concept of Sovereignty (Politische*

The Kelsenian concept of the state, especially in its democratic form, is completely free from 'miracles', in fact from any heteronomous intervention, and indeed from anything that eludes rational criticism. Democracy is the form of government best suited to the rationalisation of the political order, which autocracy disdains. Kelsen's association of relativism with democracy has implications for his characterisation of the political leader. While autocracy tends to confer absolute power on leaders, in democracy their selection is associated with rational considerations, and reflects only a relative value, subject to regular reassessments or penalties. A leader, like everything else in a democracy, is subject to criticism.[27]

> In the system of *democratic* ideology, the problem of creating leaders is at the centre of rational consideration, and leadership is definitely not an absolute but only a relative value. The leader is a 'leader' only for a certain period and in certain respects; he is otherwise an equal comrade and is subject to criticism. From this there also follows the *publicity* of government actions, in contrast to the principle of *confidentiality* in autocracies. And from the fact that in autocracies leaders are transcendent to the community, while in democracies they are immanent, follows the characteristic consequence that in autocracies the person governing is always regarded as over, not under, the social order, and is therefore essentially irresponsible, *whereas the responsibility of the leader is a specific characteristic of real democracy.*[28]

This relativism with respect to values should not be interpreted as a negation of them. For Kelsen, they do play a certain part in the formation of political opinions, especially in the parliamentary arena. But when one value is preferred to another, that is not a cognitive process in action, it is a decision-making process that follows clearly-stated rules.[29] The guarantee of the democratic character of the decision resides in the procedure that precedes and enables it. For Kelsen, this reasoning

---

Theologie. Vier Kapitel zur Lehre von der Souveränität, 1922), trans. G. Schwab, Chicago, University of Chicago Press, 2005, p. 42, my emphasis.

27 Cf. H. Kelsen, 'State-form and world-outlook', especially p. 105.

28 H. Kelsen, *Vom Wesen und Wert der Demokratie*, 1929, in M. Jestaedt and O. Lepsius (eds) *Verteidigung der Demokratie*, Tübingen: Mohr Siebeck, 2006, pp. 216–217 (original emphasis).

29 'Kelsen's value-relativism naturally implies no denial of values or making light of value-attitudes; it is simply a matter of regarding them as decisions, as something that cannot be demonstrated in purely cognitive fashion. Kelsen's pure positivism and his relativist theory of value are not unrealistic and neutral in their pragmatic consequences; they lead, rather, to a critique of ideology, to an understanding of value-pluralism, to the postulate of tolerance, to a pluralistic democracy based on the free play of ideas in the self-correcting dialectic of clashing opinions within the field of legal development. They do this, however, without the fiction that in the process we shall simply apprehend "correct" law that has somehow been previously given.' O. Weinberger, 'Introduction: Hans Kelsen as Philosopher', in O. Weinberger (ed.), *Hans Kelsen: Essays...*, pp. xxv – xxvi.

establishes a relationship between relativism and procedural or formal democracy. Democracy is primarily a form of government[30] that respects codified procedures. The will of the state is created in the institutionalised confrontation of opinions and diverse interests, with no value being able to claim superior legitimacy. In this perspective, the distinction between form and substance disappears, since the winning rule is closely tied to the democratic decision procedures that made it possible. As Kelsen sees it, antiproceduralist diatribes arguing that too much formalism removes the substance of politics, have an antidemocratic bent, because they neglect the driving forces of the democratic process.

> There is [...] no better means to obstruct the movement for democracy, to pave the way for autocracy, to dissuade the people from their desire for participation in government, than to depreciate the definition of democracy as a procedure by the argument that it is 'formalistic', to make the people believe that their desire is fulfilled if the government acts in their interest, that they have achieved the longed for democracy if they have a government for the people. The political doctrine which furnishes the appropriate ideology for such a tendency emphasises the point that the essence of democracy is a government in the interest of the mass of the people, that the participation of the people in the government is of secondary importance.[31]

The Kelsenian belief in the procedures and the proper functioning of institutions collided with the reality of parliaments and party systems in practice (especially in Weimar), which from 1929 onwards, confronted situations of institutional blockage in which the formation of compromises became increasingly difficult. Formal democracy, kept in an equilibrium by rules and procedures, found it difficult to oppose arguments in favour of a 'true democracy', arguments that sometimes – in particular, in Carl Schmitt – took the form of plebiscitary democracy.

Democracy and Religion

A certain reflection on the relations between democracy and religion flows from Kelsen's thinking about relativism. He asserts that no connection or compatibility between them can be established. This issue is the subject of a chapter in 'Foundations of Democracy' (1955), in which Kelsen discusses some attempts at 'democratic theology', including those of the protestants Emil Brunner (1889–1966) and Reinhold Niebuhr (1892–1971) and of the Catholic, Jacques Maritain (1882–1973), which confer on democracy a foundation or a Christian origin. Kelsen vigorously denies the validity of this perspective, since in his view,

---

30 H. Kelsen, 'Foundations of democracy', p. 5.
31 ibid.

justifications for democracy cannot be metaphysical: democracy is not achieved by applying unimpeachable values, in this case values conveyed to us by religion. In this chapter in 'Foundations of Democracy' devoted to the relationship between democracy and religion, Kelsen also examines Maritain's 'democratic theology', according to which the democratic ideal is rooted in evangelical inspiration. In *Christianity and Democracy* (1945), Maritain asserted that democracy's fulfilment required that it become Christian.[32] According to Kelsen, it is difficult to imagine how the gospel can serve as the metaphysical source of democracy, since Christianity, as a religion, claims to be indifferent to political systems.[33]

In Kelsen's view, a scientific theory of democracy can be established only within the limits of a rationality that matches necessary means to relative ends. Justifications of this kind of government can come only from a choice of non-absolute values, as a result of a prior decision. Democracy can be established only if the majority aspires to a form of government that attains both the values of equality and those of individual liberty. Instead of giving these values a transcendent status, Kelsen connects them to decisions, and holds up to society the 'gravity' of the directions it chooses to take. Given the importance of these choices, there is a strong temptation to hand them over to an external authority. Religion is an obvious candidate. Kelsen thought that the fear that arose from such decisions explains this attraction to metaphysics, religion and natural law, and therefore, the rejection and distrust of positivist and relativist doctrines. Christian theology, with its 'metaphysical' justification for democracy, illustrates this. The Kelsenian idea of democracy cannot cope with this reliance on metaphysics. Such reliance would imperil the whole Kelsenian edifice, since he bases democracy on immanent and ever contestable values.

Democracy and Economics

Parallel to Kelsen's reflections on the religious foundation of democracy, which in his view is contestable, is his discussion in 'Foundations of Democracy' of the relationship between democracy and economics. He considers, in turn, the arguments of those who associate democracy either with capitalism or with socialism, concluding in the end that no such connection can be conceptually established. He dismisses each of this pair of conceptions.

> Regarding this problem, two contradictory doctrines are advocated in our time. According to the one, democracy is possible only together with capitalism. It is the specific form of government congenial to this economic system [...]. According to the other doctrine, democracy, that is to say, true democracy,

---

32 London: Centenary Press, 1945.

33 H. Kelsen, 'Foundations of democracy', p. 63.

is possible only within the economic system of socialism, whereas under capitalism only a 'formal' or sham democracy can exist.[34]

Let us look first at the Marxist doctrine, in which democracy is possible only in a socialist economy. From this point of view, only socialism is in a position to achieve the material interest of the people. But the interest of the people is here confused with the will of the people. In the Marxist perspective, the economic sphere is preeminent, and political phenomena such as the state and related norms are merely the superstructure of the relations of production. So if, in a capitalist society, the minority have most of the means of production, that minority necessarily becomes politically dominant which, in the Marxist approach, is incompatible with the rules of democracy understood as the government of the majority for the majority. Only nationalisation of the means of production enables the majority to become economically – and therefore politically – dominant, and thus to establish a real democracy.[35] But thinking that for this reason only a socialist government is democratic is, in Kelsen's view, highly problematic, for it assumes that the will of the people is essentially directed towards achieving its economic interests, and that demands related to that quest are dominant and take precedence over all other kinds of claim. But history shows that nationalist and religious ideals have generated enthusiasm and fanaticism, in spite of the large economic sacrifices or restrictions that they involve.[36] Kelsen's refutation of Marxist critiques of formal democracy is clearly saturated with relativism: he privileges no priority whatsoever in the establishment of values, which is to be determined in the democratic process. The value of material equality is one value among others.

Kelsen then discusses the arguments that establish a necessary connection between capitalism and democracy, and finds that this relationship is often transferred into another discussion, that of the relations between the rule of law and the capitalist system. This linkage is used to show that a capitalist economy alone is compatible with the rule of law, because the rule of law preserves the fundamental liberties that are inherent in this system of political organisation. But Kelsen responds to that argument by pointing out that the rule of law does not assume any restriction on the activities of the legislative power. In other words, the rule of law does not necessarily guarantee economic liberty, only a degree of predictability in the application of the law by administrative and judicial bodies.[37]

---

34   ibid., p. 68.

35   ibid., p. 69.

36   ibid., p. 70.

37   'The effect of the rule of law is the rationalization of the activity of the government, that is, the processes of creation and application of the law. Its aim is not freedom but security, security in the field of law, *Rechtssicherheit*, as it is called in German jurisprudence. If the problem of democracy and economics is approached from the point of view of rationalization and security, it must be

Kelsen's twin refutation of Marxist and capitalist perspectives, each of which sees itself as essentially democratic, draws our attention back to the intimate relation that is woven by Kelsen between democracy and relativism.[38]

---

admitted that it is just the rationalization of the economic process and economic security at which socialism, with its planned economy, is driving, in opposition to capitalism which, with its anarchy of production, is far from guaranteeing economic security.' ibid., p. 78.

38 'The result of the foregoing analysis is that the attempts at showing an essential connection between freedom and property, as all other attempts to establish a closer relationship of democracy with capitalism rather than with socialism or even the exclusive compatibility of democracy with capitalism, have failed. Hence our thesis stands that democracy as a political system is not necessarily attached to a definite economic system.' ibid., p. 94.

chapter two | the instruments of political liberty

For Hans Kelsen, democracy does not require axiological justification; it is not based on intangible values. What, then, distinguishes it from other forms of government? For Kelsen, it is respect for the principle of autonomy or self-determination that constitutes the dividing line between regimes. People live in a democracy insofar as they submit to rules that they have chosen. His distinction between forms of government is based on the principle of political liberty, thus creating two ideal types: autocracy and democracy. A person is politically free if he is subject to his own will and not to a heteronomous or alien will. In a democratic regime, the will expressed in the legal order is identical to the will of the subjects. However, if subjected to an autocracy, they remain excluded from the creation of norms, and harmony between the order and their will is no longer assured.

Like Jean-Jacques Rousseau, Kelsen asks: 'How is it possible to be subject to a social order and still be free?'[1] Following Rousseau's example, Kelsen strips, from the concept of freedom, its originally accepted 'negative' meaning – the absence of restraint – to give it a 'positive' political sense.[2] Liberty becomes the 'self-determination of the individual by participating in the creation of the social order. Political freedom is liberty, and liberty is autonomy'.[3] The act of constituting a state and its legal system goes hand in hand with a metamorphosis of the meaning of liberty. The liberty of the individual, i.e. the liberty of the state of nature, is replaced by the claim of the sovereignty of the people – their power to determine the rules that they are subjected to – in accordance with the principle of autonomy,[4] the primary principle of democracy. For Kelsen, in democratic societies, legality replaces natural liberty.[5] Although Kelsen and Rousseau share this search for the

---

1   H. Kelsen, *General Theory of Law and State*, trans. A. Wedberg, Cambridge, Mass.: Harvard University Press, 1945, p. 285.

2   ibid., pp. 284–285.

3   ibid., p. 285.

4   Cf. ibid.

5   'From the epistemological point of view, if a society different from a natural system is ever possible, there must be alongside natural legality a specifically social legality. Causal law opposes norms. Originally, from the point of view of nature, freedom means negation of the social; from the point of view of society, it means negation of natural (causal) legality (free will). "Returning to nature" (or to "natural" freedom) just means losing social bonding. The ascent to society (or to social freedom) means freedom from natural legality. This contradiction is lost only when "freedom" is the expression of a specific – namely, social (i.e. ethical-political and legal-governmental) legality; and when the contrast between nature and society is a contrast of two different legalities and thus of two different directions of observation.' H. Kelsen, *Vom Wesen und Wert der Demokratie*, 1929,

meaning of the concept of liberty in a system of a binding order, they diverge on the ways in which the will of the state is formed. In contrast to Rousseau, Kelsen does not exclude conflict from democratic procedures.

Kelsen treats the notion of the 'general will' as an image, and he frequently prefers to use, instead, the idea of the social order.[6] In the Kelsenian definition of democracy, the idea of liberty, in its positive sense, is primary, and the notion of equality plays only a strictly formal role. Equality enters into the account only in this way: 'Because all should be as free as possible, therefore equally free, all should participate in equal measure in the formation of the will of the state'.[7] Thus Kelsen is compelled to resist the Marxist currents that try to replace formal democracy with a mode of social organisation that is considered more egalitarian and more just. With that change of direction, democracy loses its meaning; it is no longer essentially characterised by political liberty or self-determination. A Kelsenian democracy must leave open and uncertain the choice of values, and the modes of organising and distributing resources. So the hijacking of the meaning of democracy by Marxist thinking is judged with great severity by Kelsen, as is shown by this sentence:

> This terminological manipulation has, if not actually the intention, nevertheless the serious result that the great legitimating force and the whole sense of value that, thanks to the ideology of freedom, the watchword of democracy carries, are siphoned off to prop up a system of blatant political dictatorship.[8]

According to Kelsen, a democratic regime assumes that individuals are subject to the rules that are chosen by the majority, and that means that the norms do not come from a single will but are created in a 'decentralised' way. Particularly in his *General Theory of Law and State*, Kelsen reflects on the relationship between the democratic and autocratic types of state, and centralised and decentralised organisational forms. He distinguishes between two kinds of centralisation (and decentralisation): static – i.e. related to 'the territorial validity of the norms' – and dynamic – i.e. related to the ways that the norms are created and implemented. While static decentralisation goes with a territorial division of the state into provinces, cantons, departments, etc., dynamic decentralisation means that the formation and implementation of the will of the state are carried out by many people. In Kelsen's

---

in M. Jestaedt and O. Lepsius (eds) *Verteidigung der Demokratie*, Tübingen: Mohr Siebeck, 2006, p. 155.

6   'Democracy is the idea of a form of government or of society in which the communal will is formed, or – dropping the image – the social order is created, by those subjected to it: the people.' ibid., p. 162.

7   ibid., p. 220.

8   ibid., p. 221.

mind, although democracy necessarily implies a dynamic decentralisation, it does not logically presuppose a static decentralisation. So a parliamentary democracy could be conceptually compatible with territorial centralisation, and an autocracy could live with territorial decentralisation. But in practice, a territorial division into partly autonomous entities does not allow an autocracy to operate effectively, because the delegation to representatives weakens autocratic control. Besides, democracy tends to flourish better in decentralised regimes, in which the territory is administratively divided up. Democracy demands conformity between the rules that are applied to subjects and those subjects' will, and static decentralisation is certainly more geared up to producing this equivalence or an approximation to it.[9] However, while legislative processes should approximate the democratic ideal, insofar as possible meeting the rule of self-determination, administrative and judicial implementation need not be democratised. In Kelsen's view, legislation and execution are very different processes. While the creation of general norms is subject to the principle of political liberty, implementation must satisfy the need for equality of treatment and therefore cannot vary or fluctuate.[10] Democratisation of implementation and administration detracts from predictability; it 'can only take place at the expense of the substantive intensity of the legislative function.'[11]

Deliberative Institutions

After Kelsen has established the principle of autonomy or political liberty as the ultimate foundation of democracy, he examines democratic reality and its inability to reach that ideal in practice. One could even say that the starting point of his reflections on democracy in these interwar years was the necessary limits imposed on pure democracy in modern states. It is especially in terms of this antithesis between idea (or ideology) and reality, that he thought about the institutions of democracy, particularly parliamentary democracy.[12] In his ideal model, democracy

---

9   H. Kelsen, *General Theory of Law and State*, p. 306.

10 Cf. Hans Kelsen, 'Geschworengericht und Demokratie. Das Prinzip der Legalität' (1929), in A. J. Merkl and A. Verdross (eds), *Die Wiener Rechtstheoretische Schule*, Wien, Europa Verlag, 1968, pp. 1777–1779; cf. also Hans Kelsen, 'Demokratisierung der Verwaltung', (1921) in Merkl and Verdross (eds), *Die Wiener...*, pp. 1581–1591.

11 H. Kelsen, *Vom Wesen und Wert...*, p. 208. 'Implementation is in essence subject to the idea of legality, and at some stage of government decision-making, the idea of legality comes into conflict with that of democracy.' ibid., p. 205.

12 'The metamorphosis of freedom thinking leads from the idea to the reality of democracy. Its essence can be recognized only in the strange and (especially for the problem of democracy) characteristic contrast between ideology and reality. Any number of misunderstandings continually recur in debates about democracy because the opposing sides only ever take into consideration one aspect of the phenomenon – one side considers the idea, the other the reality – whereas no one grasps it

envisages the social and legal order as the product of the will of the dominated ('*Unterworfenen*'). But this ideal identity between subject and object of domination in a democratic order turns out to be unrealistic, for the reasons that Kelsen listed in 1927 in his article on '*Demokratie*.'[13] In the first place, the different physical and psychic characteristics of elected officials ('age, gender, mental and moral health, etc.') give them all unequal power in the formation of the state's will. Second, their various levels of interest in public affairs give them unequal political influence. Third, majority rule does not fully respect the will of the majority. Fourth, the division of labour justifying a system of representation gives the representatives greater power. Fifth, the implementation of democratic laws takes place through a bureaucracy that is not chosen by democratic means. And finally, political parties, which are the intermediaries between civil and political society, are not always formed in a democratic way.

Kelsen defines actual democracy in the light of the inevitable limitations of the democratic ideal. Even if democracy must give up the ideal of autonomy, in the sense of everyone's equal participation in the formation of the will of the state, what can it do in order to approach this utopia, keeping in mind the constraints of the modern state? This question focuses attention on institutions, and as means of forming the will of the state Kelsen pays special attention to majority rule, political parties, and representative democracy. These institutions may violate the ideal of autonomy, but according to Kelsen they are nevertheless decisive and very valuable instruments in modern democracies, because they make it possible to approximate a perfect democracy.

Majority Rule

In the ideal of political liberty, the rules of the social and political order come from the unanimous will of the members of the state. However, this principle of self-determination has to be restricted, because it is not possible to meet the requirements of unanimity without giving up on any changes to a given order. So the inevitable existence of conflicts and divergent points of view within a state imposes limitations on self-determination, i.e. on respect for the principle of unanimity. According to Kelsen, majority rule is most likely to ensure maximum autonomy while allowing changes in the social order. Thus the principle of majority rule is part of the change in the meaning given to the ideal of liberty that is necessary in order to constitute a social and political order.

The greatest possible degree of individual liberty, and that means, the greatest possible approximation to the ideal of self-determination compatible with the

---

in its entirety, seeing the reality in the light of the elevating ideology, and the ideology with a view to the reality that supports it.' ibid., p. 162.

13 In Merkl and Verdross (eds), *Die Wiener...*, pp. 1743–1776.

existence of a social order, is guaranteed by the principle that a change of the social order requires the consent of the simple majority of the subjects of that order.[14]

Political Parties

In Kelsen's view, in order for political liberty to be realised, society needs to develop instruments that enable it to express its preferences effectively. Political parties play the essential role of transmitting these preferences. Particularly in his writings in the 1920s, Kelsen thought about democracy only in terms of a 'party state' that necessarily implied collective groups that fit between civil and political society.[15] In his reflections after the First World War, he admired and promoted the new and growing role that, especially in Austria and Germany, was being taken by political parties in constitutional transformation.[16] For Kelsen, political life does not exist without the parties that are democracy's primary interlocutors in the search for compromises between majorities and minorities. So it seems natural to him that they should be given legal status and a place in the constitution, as bodies taking part in the formation of the will of the state. In *Vom Wesen und Wert der Demokratie* (*Democracy: Its Nature and Value*), Kelsen sketches a program to enhance political parties, some aspects of which we shall discuss later. In his view, by representing the interests in civil society and by thus enabling conformity between the rules society adopts and the wishes of the majority, political parties play an influential part in heeding the principle of autonomy. That finally explains the important place that parties occupy in his theory of democracy. Like Alexis de Tocqueville, Kelsen believed that isolated individuals have little weight in political life, unless they join together in groups and associations.[17]

---

14 H. Kelsen, *General Theory of Law and State*, p. 286.

15 'Only self-deception or hypocrisy can maintain that democracy is possible without political parties. [..] Democracy is necessarily and inevitably a party state.' H. Kelsen, *Vom Wesen und Wert...*, p. 167.

16 E. Pikart, 'Die Rolle der Parteien im deutschen konstitutionellen System vor 1914,' in E.-W. Böckenförde (ed.), *Moderne deutsche Verfassungsgeschichte (1815–1918)*, Köln: Kiepenheuer & Witsch, 1972, p. 258.

17 The importance for democratic life that Kelsen accords to the formation of political parties, and to associations more generally, is Tocquevillean in spirit. Cf. H. Kelsen, *Vom Wesen und Wert der Demokratie*, pp. 165–166, and A. de Tocqueville, *De la Démocratie en Amérique* (1835–1840), Paris: Garnier Flammarion, 1981, in particular, Vol. II, Part II, Chapter V, 'De l'usage que les Américains font de l'association dans la vie civile' ('Of the Use That Americans Make of Association in Civil Life'). Cf. also Richard Saage, *Politische Ideengeschichte in demokratie-theoretischer Absicht: das Beispiel Hans Kelsens und Max Adlers in der Zwischenkriegszeit*, Leipzig: Verlag der Sächsischer Akademie der Wissenschaften, 2003, p. 13.

The close relationship that Kelsen establishes between partisan pluralism and democratic life is most clearly visible in an essay he published in Geneva in 1934, called *La Dictature de parti* (The Party Dictatorship).[18] Here he distinguishes democratic regimes from Nazism and Bolshevism on the basis of the presence or absence of a multiparty system. The democratic process resides in the confrontation between opposing interest groups, represented most effectively by political parties. The appreciation of partisan organisations and Kelsen's enthusiasm in including them in his democratic theory, single him out from other constitutionalists, particularly at Weimar, who did not share his optimism about the party system and the place that it occupied in parliamentary arenas. While some jurists after 1918, for example Max Weber and Carl Schmitt, remained fearful about the emergence of party organisations, not only did Kelsen not fear them, he regarded them as 'one of the most important elements of true democracy,' because they ensure that individuals, grouped in accordance with their opinions, have an influence on the management of public affairs.[19] For Kelsen, the emergence of political parties and their inclusion in the constitution, follows from a rationalisation of power, an integral part of modern democratic states. This equation that he formulated between democracy and the party state is absent from today's rhetoric, which seems to echo the antiparliamentary criticisms of the interwar period, with their repudiation of the party system and of interfaces between state and civil society more generally. This rhetoric would make 'treason by representation' a slogan, which was something that Kelsen in his political works steadfastly resisted.

The Parliamentary Arena

Political liberty (or the principle of self-determination), which is limited because of majority rule, is also limited because of the necessary division of labour that affects the political sphere. For issues relating to competence, it is mainly the elected representatives (MPs) in parliamentary chambers who determine the content and contours of the political order. Just as majority rule is a compromise between the ideal of self-determination and the necessity of restricting the requirement of unanimity, representative democracy reconciles the claim of the principle of autonomy with the necessary division of labour.[20] In parliamentary systems, the requirement of 'self-determination' is limited to the choice of representatives, i.e. to the formation of a legislative body. Because it restricts citizens' effective participation, parliamentarianism does not perfectly satisfy the democratic principle. However, according to Kelsen, these two notions have many

---

18 H. Kelsen, *La Dictature de parti* (The Party Dictatorship), Paris: Institut international de droit public, 1934.

19 H. Kelsen, *Vom Wesen und Wert...*, p. 166.

20 ibid., p. 39.

links, including historical, ideological and 'pragmatic' ones. 'The fight against autocracy in the late eighteenth and early nineteenth centuries was essentially a struggle for parliamentarianism.'[21] Representative government has generated expectations, which are those that democracy brought in its wake; among them, popular participation, through representation, in the formation of the will of the state. In addition, the parliamentary system seems to be the most appropriate way to realise the democratic ideal, given that direct democracy is impractical in modern states.

Although Kelsen's reflections on democratic institutions raise some general questions, they are also historically situated. His advocacy of parliamentary democracy in the 1920s has to be seen in the context of a crisis of European parliamentarianism. In this climate of strong opposition to and distrust of Parliament, Kelsen published successively *Allgemeine Staatslehre* (*General Theory of the State*, 1925), *Das Problem des Parlamentarismus* (*The Problem of Parliamentarianism*, 1925), and *Vom Wesen und Wert der Demokratie* (*Democracy: Its Nature and Value*, 1929), in which he denounced the most radical forms of anti-parliamentarianism. Several telling critiques of parliamentary institutions appeared in the 1920s. In 1928 a collection of articles entitled *L'Évolution actuelle du régime représentatif* (*Current Developments in Representative Government*) was published in Geneva. With contributions from five authors, English, French, Italian and German (Harold J. Laski, Charles Borgeaud, Fernand Larnaude, Gaetano Mosca, and Moritz Julius Bonn), this report examined 'the crisis that parliamentarianism is going through [...] in almost every state, [as well] as the criticisms and [...] attacks to which it is being subjected from very different quarters.'[22] The magnitude of the crisis can be seen in the article by Fernand Larnaude, which lists several contemporary writings that denounce the shortcomings of parliamentary institutions, with titles such as 'The Decline of Our Institutions,' 'The Diseases of Democracy,' and 'How To Improve the Parliamentary Machine.'[23] In the face of the most radical criticisms, Kelsen remade the case for parliamentary institutions and a certain conception of democracy.[24] He responded specifically to Carl Schmitt's *The Crisis of Parliamentary Democracy*, the first version of which was published

---

21 ibid., p. 37.

22 Union interparlementaire, 'Introduction,' in H. J. Laski *et al.*, *L'Évolution actuelle du régime représentative: cinq réponses à une enquête de l'Union interparlementaire*, Genève: Payot, 1928, p. 5.

23 F. Larnaude, 'L'Évolution actuelle du régime représentative', in ibid., p. 42.

24 Kelsen was not alone in opposing antiparliamentary arguments in the interwar period. To cite one example, Hermann Heller and Rudolf Smend also tried to rescue parliamentary democracy from disillusionment; cf. S. Baume, 'Le Parlement face à ses adversaires. La réplique allemande au désenchantement démocratique dans l'entre-deux-guerres', *Revue française de science politique*, December 2006, 56, pp. 985–998.

in 1923.[25] Schmitt here took the view that the nineteenth-century parliamentary ideal had been widely betrayed. Parliament was no longer the place where independent representatives of particular interests confronted each other, or where the best arguments were enough to sway the debaters. It had become instead the place where decisions in line with the instructions of parties were registered. Parliamentarianism had departed from its founding 'myths': the assumptions of publicity ('*Öffentlichkeit*'), of free competition of opinions, and of trust in discussion.[26] According to Schmitt, the conditions for realising parliamentarianism in democracies had disappeared. Secret deliberations steered by interests had replaced free and public discussion,[27] so parliamentary institutions had become void or 'illegitimate.'

Among the rejoinders that were formulated to defend parliamentary institutions in their democratic legitimacy in spite of their imperfections, Kelsen put forward perhaps one of the most effective arguments. He rejected Schmitt's antiparliamentary critique not by asserting that Parliament actually lived up to the optimal conditions for deliberation, but by assigning to Parliament, and to democracy, the purpose not of producing 'political truth', but of providing the best possible deliberation. This counter-assumption – formulated by Kelsen in *Allgemeine Staatslehre* (1925), *Das Problem des Parlamentarismus* (1925), and *Vom Wesen und Wert der Demokratie* (1929) – could still today serve to oppose critiques saying that Parliament is a non-democratic institution because of its 'deliberative imperfections'. For Kelsen, it is not the mission of Parliament to achieve an ideal of truth; it does not have to guarantee that it has made the best choice in order to be legitimate. Democracy in general and parliamentarianism in particular, are not systems that produce political truths. The purpose and meaning of Parliaments are to seek to create compromises among divergent values and interests.[28] Through this relativistic reasoning, Kelsen undermines one part of the antiparliamentarian criticism based on the idea of the betrayal of a deliberative ideal. Parliamentary democracies do not pursue 'absolute truths' or a 'true' will of the state; they seek a middle line between majority and minority interests.

---

25 C. Schmitt, *The Crisis of Parliamentary Democracy,* trans. E. Kennedy, Cambridge, MA.:MIT Press, 1988.

26 According to Schmitt, Parliament also fell short in its mission of selecting elites: C. Schmitt, Preface to the Second Edition (1926): 'On the Contradiction between Parliamentarism and Democracy', in *The Crisis of Parliamentary Democracy*, (a translation of *Die geistesgeschichtliche Lage des heutigen Parliamentarismus*, 1923), trans. E. Kennedy, ibid., p. 4

27 C. Schmitt, 'Practical consequences of the fundamental idea of the parliamentary system (representation, the public, discussion),' in *Constitutional Theory*, (a translation of *Verfassungslehre*, Munich and Leipzig: Duncker und Humblot, 1928), trans. J. Seitzer (ed.), Durham and London: Duke University Press, 2008, ch. 24, section III.

28 H. Kelsen, *Allgemeine Staatslehre* (*General Theory of the State*), Berlin: Julius Springer, 1925, p. 359.

In Kelsen's view, to show, as Schmitt does, that parliamentary debates and the instruments that assist the formation of opinion – newspapers – do not result in 'true legislation' does not amount to a serious objection. Nothing could be more mistaken than to attribute to liberal democracy an 'absolute and metaphysical conception of the world', for its conception is in fact critical and relativistic.[29]

Schmitt's mistrust of parliamentary democracy was not unique or even rare in Weimar; it was symptomatic of the concerns provoked by the democratic institutions of representation. In Germany this apprehensiveness was palpable not only in conservative circles but also, although moderately, among some democrats like Hugo Preuss[30] and Max Weber. In the interwar period, Schmitt simply radicalised this wariness about Parliament. Although the 1920s debate about the legitimacy of parliamentary systems involved a number of European countries, it was particularly salient in Germany, precisely because of the profound crisis in Parliament and the party system.[31] Even before Kelsen lived in Cologne (1930–1933), in the last years of the Weimar Republic he was a very attentive observer of German political life, and he participated in the high-level debate on political institutions. As shown by his publications and the strong reactions to them, he had a significant role in discussions on the theory of the state. After the First World War, the spirited controversies referred to as a 'dispute about methods' included confrontations particularly among Kelsen, Hermann Heller, Erich Kaufmann, Carl Schmitt, and Rudolf Smend. Reports of the meetings of the Association of

---

29 H. Kelsen, *Das Problem des Parlamentarismus*, Wien, Leipzig: Wilhelm Braumüller, 1925, pp. 39–40.

30 In November 1918, Hugo Preuss (1860–1925) was appointed Secretary of the Interior, and was responsible for drafting the constitution of the Weimar Republic. He was also a founding member of the German Democratic Party (DDP). From February to June 1919 he was Minister of the Interior. In 1920 he was elected as a DDP Deputy in the Prussian Landtag and worked on the new Prussian Land Constitution that came into effect in November 1920.

31 For some observers in France, the Weimar Republic became in the twentieth-century a laboratory for reflections and controversies about the institution of parliament. Many analysts paid particular attention to the dysfunctioning of the party system, believed to be an important source of the crisis in the Reichstag (Parliament), which became fatal in 1933: 'so the problem of the parliamentary coalition is at the centre of German politics. The Bismarckian framework having collapsed, only the parties were left as political agents. Surprised by the defeat, and furnished with new labels after hastily overhauling their programs, the parties were not transformed by the Revolution'. E. Vermeil, *La Constitution de Weimar et le principe de la démocratie allemande*, Strasbourg: Libr. Istra, 1923, p. 435. Also consider C. Eisenmann, 'Bonn et Weimar, deux Constitutions de l'Allemagne' (1950), in *Écrits de théorie du droit, de droit constitutionnel et d'idées politiques*, Paris, Panthéon-Assas, 2002, p. 483. In 1928, C. Schmitt in his *Constitutional Theory*, p.85 cited the analysis of E. Vermeil: 'In his work on the Weimar Constitution, E. Vermeil (Strassburg [sic] 1923, especially p. 223) portrayed the contradictions within the National Assembly and the absence there of a "homogeneous and coherent theory".'

German Law Teachers ('*Vereinigung der Deutschen Staatsrechtslehrer*') from 1925 to 1929 echo these debates.[32] The dispute related to methodological issues, but was highly politicised. In fact, the full name of this dispute was '*Methoden oder Richtungsstreit der Staatsrechtslehre*' ('dispute about methods or directions in the theory of public law'), and in it conflicting perspectives were opposed: authoritarian and democratic, liberal and statist, positivist and antipositivist. The Kelsenian response to the disenchantment with parliamentary institutions was developed partly in this historico-discursive context.

Compromise: An Ideal of the Relations between Majority and Minority

With Kelsen defining democracy by its ability to approach – if not to realise – the ideal of political liberty, he is necessarily concerned with the relations between majorities and minorities. Like Moritz Julius Bonn (1873–1965)[33], Kelsen perceived in the issue of the protection of minorities, one of the major challenges for modern democracies. Relations between the majority and the minority cannot be domination of the latter by the former; if that were the case, the principle of self-determination would be violated. The relations that become established between the majority and the minority should not be oppression of one by the other, even though they clearly favour the majority. What protects the minority group in a democratic order? For Kelsen, the existence of the majority presupposes that of the minority. The minority cannot be deprived of their rights without them leaving the democratic process, and by ceasing to take part in it they would compromise the whole system of representation.[34]

---

32 The Association was formed in 1922 with Heinrich Triepel as its president. Among its members were a number of German-language jurists, notably Hugo Preuss, Rudolf Smend, Erich Kaufmann, Carl Schmitt, Gerhard Anschütz, Richard Thoma, Otto Koellreutter, Rudolf Laun, Hermann Heller, Walter Jellinek, Fritz Stier-Somlo, Ernst von Hippel, Erwin Jacobi, Hans Nawiasky, Edgar Tatarin-Tarnheyden, Hans Kelsen, Fritz Sander, and Thomas Fleiner-Gerster. The Association's meetings stopped in 1931, and restarted in 1949. Cf. the detailed observations of C.-M. Herrera, *Théorie juridique et politique chez Hans Kelsen*, Paris: Kimé, 1997, pp. 85–96.

33 During the interwar period, Kelsen was not the only one reflecting on the relations between minorities and democracy. In 1925, Moritz Julius Bonn wrote in *Die Krisis der europäischen Demokratie* (*The Crisis of European Democracy*), München: Meyer and Jessen, 1925, p. 127: 'The chief internal problem of parliamentary democracy – of the form of democracy, against which almost all attacks are directed – is the problem of the protection of minorities.' For the pre-Weimar period, cf. also G. Jellinek, *Das Recht der Minoritäten*, Wien: A. Hölder, 1898.

34 H. Kelsen, *Vom Wesen und Wert...*, pp. 193–194.

A dictatorship of the majority over the minority is not even possible in the long run, if only because a minority, reduced to having absolutely no influence, will finally abandon a participation that is merely formal, and therefore worthless, or even harmful for it in terms of forming the communal will; thereby, it will take away from the majority its very character as a majority, since by definition, a majority presupposes a minority.[35]

The minority should be protected so that the social order resulting from the will of the majority, will not totally contradict the interests of the minority group. Clearly the idea of a contract between the majority and the minority is insinuating itself here, a contract that compels the majority not to systematically act with violence against the minority,[36] and compels the minority to tolerate, in accordance with democratic rules, norms that it would not itself have chosen. For Kelsen, the development of compromise between the majority and minority parties is a sign of democratic vitality.

In a chapter in *Allgemeine Staatslehre* that Kelsen specifically dedicates to forms of government ('Staatsformen'), including the polar pair autocracy-democracy, he establishes as a distinguishing criterion, the type of political integration that the state adopts.[37] 'Dynamic' integration characterises democracy, while 'static' integration goes more with states of the autocratic kind. A dynamic integration of a plurality assumes that the 'harmony' that reigns in the relevant system, results from constant renewals of the arrangements between the majority and the minority, in contrast to autocratic regimes, which do not tolerate negotiations in the distribution of power. In this treatise, Kelsen gives a very special place to the idea of compromise,[38] linked to the idea of a contract between the majority and the minority. Given that in Kelsen's view there is no harmonious society with a spontaneous conciliation of interests, neither the regulation of divergent interests nor ultimately social integration, can be achieved except by negotiation that is always provisional. According to Kelsen, harmony in a political community can result only from a renewable compromise between the different actors in the plurality.[39] Moreover, his definition of compromise emphasises the intimate bond woven between this concept and the rule of self-determination, the first principle of democratic government:

---

35   ibid., p. 196.

36   Cf. H. Kelsen, *Allgemeine Staatslehre*, p. 324.

37   ibid., pp. 326–327.

38   'If the state can function only by the cooperation of two or more bodies with conflicting interests from any angle whatsoever, then it must move in the direction of compromise. The tendency to compromise – which we shall return to later – must therefore be recognized as an essential feature of democracy'. ibid., p. 259.

39   ibid., p. 324.

Compromise means: to replace what breaks connections with what makes them. Every exchange, every contract is a compromise, for to compromise means to tolerate. All social integration is ultimately possible only through compromise. Indeed the majority itself can only arise through such a compromise. The derogatory, contemptuous judgement that is not infrequently expressed about the principle of compromise and about an attitude inclined to compromise, comes neither from the ideology of liberty nor from thinking about self-determination.[40]

In Kelsen's thinking, compromises appear as agents of stability in democratic regimes, because they allow the expression of 'political emotions' in the public sphere, which if they are driven back to the private sphere, might well eventually lead to violent reactions, rebellions, or even revolutions. In autocratic regimes, political stability rests on the repression of political emotions 'into a sphere comparable to the subconscious in individual psychology.'[41] Kelsen takes a cautious step into the field of psychoanalysis in order to emphasise the pacific virtues of compromises based on the recognition, expression and reconciliation of conflicts.[42]

For parliamentary compromises to be an instrument of political stability, the representation of political forces must be as finely tuned as possible. Therefore Kelsen defends proportional rather than majority electoral systems. His case for proportional representation coincides with a particular understanding of the political body, conceived of never as a unity, but rather as a set of groups with patently contradictory opinions and values. In his view, political parties represent this diversity, by dividing up the seats in accordance with electoral strength.[43] When there are compromises that bring together most of the political forces, Kelsen does not think this is a second-best formation of the will of the state. On the contrary, it is highly valued because it provides a solution to conflict, and although naturally it does not fully meet the interests of the minority, neither is it completely contrary to them;[44] it allows an approximation to a democratic ideal. Kelsen's pursuit of reflections on the reconciliation of interests takes place, especially during the interwar period, in a climate of social division and of class warfare that showed up in the political balance. How could the class warfare that emerged in Europe be kept from threatening political life? That is the question raised by Kelsen and

---

40 ibid.

41 H. Kelsen, *Vom Wesen und Wert...*, p. 202.

42 On the relations between Kelsen and psychoanalysis, in particular Freudians, cf. R. A. Metall, *Hans Kelsen: Leben und Werk*, Wien: F. Deuticke, 1969, pp. 40–41. Cf. also H. Kelsen, 'The conception of the state and social psychology: with special reference to Freud's group theory', *International Journal of Psycho-Analysis*, 1924, vol. 5, pp. 1–38.

43 H. Kelsen, *Vom Wesen und Wert...*, p. 197.

44 H. Kelsen, *General Theory of Law and State*, p. 288.

by other writers (for example Hermann Heller[45]) who constantly thought about political institutions, particularly parliamentary institutions, with a view to getting a social plurality to coexist politically. Kelsen's scientific contribution was in theorising compromise as a mechanism for managing and resolving the conflicts that are part of democratic life. In this way, he displayed great optimism about the capacity of civil society peacefully to reconcile opposing sides – an optimism considered excessive by Carl Schmitt and all the supporters of authoritarian thinking, who seek institutional stability by a recourse to putting commanding force at the top of the state.

The Revival of the Imperative Mandate

Attempts to delegitimise Parliament are often made by referring to an imagined 'golden age' from which the institution has become definitively and fatally separated. This is the case with Carl Schmitt's antiparliamentary criticisms, which were made without considering the possibility of adapting the parliamentary system to new requirements. As Erich Kaufmann emphasised in 1958, reflecting back on the 1920s,

> institutions that arise in a particular historical situation are not inextricably linked to that concrete situation, they are on the contrary capable of adapting to different historical situations without losing their essence. This raises the question of how the parliamentary system of government arising at different times in different countries, has adapted to new situations and new needs, and how that was possible in Germany after the First World War.[46]

Proposals for reform come not from the adversaries of parliamentarianism, but from its defenders, who look to adaptations to provide new sources of legitimacy. In this respect, we shall examine Kelsen's suggestions relating to the revaluation of the role of political parties and to his reflections on parliamentarians' irresponsibility (to voters and to the courts). Some of his proposals in the late

---

45 'Will the democratic political form then stand up to class warfare, henceforth a given fact? Class warfare, when it has developed on an economic basis, does not in itself necessarily make democracy fly into pieces. This will happen only when the proletariat starts thinking that equality of political rights with its powerful opponent dooms its class warfare in democracies, so it is only then that it will appeal from democracy to dictatorship.' Hermann Heller, 'Démocratie politique et homogénéité sociale', (1928), *Cités*, 2001, vol. 6, p. 207.

46 E. Kaufmann, 'Carl Schmitt et son école: Lettre ouverte à Ernst Forsthoff', (1958), *Cités*, 2004, no. 17, p. 155. This argument was briefly developed by Richard Thoma: 'every living institution changes and undergoes functional metamorphoses and structural transformations'. 'Zur Ideologie des Parlamentarismus und der Diktatur', *Archiv für Sozialwissenschaft und Sozialpolitik*, 1925, p. 214.

1920s, relating to relations between representatives and represented, are unique in that they borrow elements of the imperative mandate. The imperative mandate can be defined as representation that conceives of deputies as the agents or the exponents of the interests of their electors. This is different from the representative mandate, which considers deputies as representing the whole nation and not as 'ambassadors' representing 'diverse and hostile interests'. The representative mandate was theorised notably by Emmanuel Sieyès and Edmund Burke.[47] With few exceptions, this second definition dominated thinking about representation after 1789.

Against this important tradition, Kelsen objects to the idea that representative government be set up in opposition to the imperative mandate. In *Vom Wesen und Wert der Demokratie*, as in *General Theory of Law and State*, he redeems some features of the imperative mandate,[48] in the connection it establishes between elected representatives and voters, or between 'mandatary' and 'mandating.' To Kelsen, the idea of representation had become a victim of mythologies transmitted by the National Constituent Assembly of 1789,[49] according to which Parliament is a body representing the people as a whole.[50] He remained, throughout his work, very suspicious of political mythologies. Representation of the nation, like the general will, appeared in the chapter on fiction: if the nation is composed of divergent, sometimes conflicting interests, it makes no sense to talk about representing the interests of *the* nation.[51] For Kelsen, the fiction of representation – the fiction of the nation – weakens the parliamentary institution, because it assigns to it a task that it cannot accomplish, and exposes Parliament to criticism generated by itself.

In Kelsen's view, representation draws on the imperative mandate, therefore

---

47 'Parliament is not a congress of ambassadors from different and hostile interests; which interests each must maintain, as an agent and advocate, against other agents and advocates; but parliament is a deliberative assembly of one nation, with one interest, that of the whole; where, not local purposes, not local prejudices, ought to guide, but the general good, resulting from the general reason of the whole.' E. Burke, *Speech to the Electors of Bristol*, 3 November 1774.

48 '[I]f some writers even declare that the *mandat impératif* is contrary to the principle of representative government, they do not present a scientific theory but advocate a political ideology. The function of this ideology is to conceal the real situation, to maintain the illusion that the legislator is the people, in spite of the fact that, in reality, the function of the people – or, more correctly formulated, of the electorate – is limited to the creation of the legislative organ.' H. Kelsen, *General Theory of Law and State*, p. 291.

49 As a member of the Assembly in 1789, Sieyès thought that every deputy should represent the whole nation.

50 H. Kelsen, *Vom Wesen und Wert...*, p. 178.

51 The formula that the member of parliament is not the representative of his electors but of the whole people, or, as some writers say of the whole State, and that therefore he is not bound by any instructions of his electors and cannot be recalled by them, is a political fiction.' H. Kelsen, *General Theory of Law and State*, p. 291.

the reforms that he suggests are attempts to strengthen the ties between voters and the representatives chosen by them. This would occur through the intervention of political parties, the role of which he wishes to enhance. For example, he suggests that voters check up on their deputies, by means of parties that would recall representatives who deviate too much from their political program.[52] But is voters' control over deputies not difficult to reconcile with the compromise activities that are so valued by Kelsen, but that require that deputies be left some room for manoeuvre? This is a question to which Kelsen does not respond. In his proposals, political parties would not only disown 'disloyal' deputies, they would also take responsibility for assigning deputies to various parliamentary committees, in order to secure the greatest degree of competence.[53] Although deputies' irresponsibility to the voters is grounds for discrediting Parliament, that is also true with regard to representatives' irresponsibility to courts, and to public bodies in general. In *Vom Wesen und Wert der Demokratie*, but also in *Allgemeine Staatslehre*, Kelsen emphasises the obsolescence of parliamentary immunity, which made sense only in a constitutional monarchy, where it allowed Parliament to hold its own in the balance of power that set it against the monarchy. Parliamentary immunity should have disappeared (or limited itself) with the rise of the Republic that established Parliament as the sovereign body. In addition to the discredit that it brings to parliaments, this immunity is incompatible with the Kelsenian concept of the hierarchy of the legal order, which does not tolerate any isolated enclaves in the judicial pyramid. Although the rather bold proposals to enhance the role of parties, and the connection that they establish between voters and deputies are now passé, the issue of parliamentary immunity often resurfaces.

In his reflections on the reform of democratic institutions, Kelsen never seriously considered any alternatives to the representation that was possible in the parliamentary arena. In his view, professional or corporate representation is not suitable for representing the diversity of the interests and the concerns that a political community contains. 'Professional interests compete with other quite dissimilar but often vital interests, e.g. religious, general ethical, and aesthetic [...]

52　'If we could decide to organize political parties by law and, by consistently applying the idea of proportional voting, leave to them the selection of the deputies to which they are entitled by their numerical strength, there would be no reason not to recognize also the right of parties, which have become an essential part of the constitution, to recall their deputies.' H. Kelsen, *Vom Wesen und Wert...*, p. 188.

53　'Reform in this direction would respond to the argument which – next after that of being alien to the people – has in recent times most often been made against parliamentary government, namely that, because of their composition, modern parliaments lack all the technical knowledge needed to make good laws in the various areas of public life. While by claiming that parliamentary will is not the same as the will of the people, we appeal to the idea of freedom that parliamentary government does not (or does not sufficiently) realize, the argument about parliaments' lack of technical competence aims in the opposite direction, namely at the division of labour.' ibid.

In what professional group could all of these vital interests be decided?'[54] These questions, not strictly connected to the professional sphere, must be confided to a non-corporate authority: in a democratic regime, to a parliament. Only it is able to grasp the issues that transcend professional corporations.[55] Caught up in multiple allegiances, citizens cannot be reduced to their corporate affiliations; they are first of all members of a state. Since it does not exhaust the range of political concerns, corporate representation can, at best, simply be juxtaposed with parliamentary representation. Partisan organisations are more likely to embrace the whole sphere of political interests. When Kelsen published the second edition of *Vom Wesen und Wert der Demokratie* in 1929, much longer than the first, he gave church-state relations as an example of the problems that cannot be understood across professional divides.[56] It was in this year that he ran into trouble as a judge of the Constitutional Court on an issue involving the Catholic principle of the indissolubility of marriage.

The Constitutional Court

In the interwar period Kelsen combined his thinking about democracy with reflections on the guarantor of the Constitution. Democracy can be established only if the compliance of the state's actions with the Constitution is provided by a constitutional review vested in a court. Kelsen's legal-political discussion of this subject is tied into a context of the development of the institutions of constitutional jurisdiction, to which he made a major contribution. He is considered to be the father of the centralised Austrian Constitutional Court. He elaborated his case for a constitutional court against many opponents who questioned the legitimacy of such a court. In 'Wesen und Entwicklung der Staatsgerichtsbarkeit' ('The Nature and Development of Court Jurisdiction', 1928),[57] the first criticism that Kelsen rejected was the incompatibility of a constitutional court with the sovereignty of Parliament. Indeed, if Parliament is regarded as the sovereign body par excellence, how can that be reconciled with a control being carried out on the legislation that it enacts? To this first criticism, Kelsen replied that Parliament, like every other public body, is subject to the Constitution, which ultimately justifies constitutional control being applied to it.[58] Such control is carried out not only on general norms

---

54 ibid., p. 190.

55 ibid., p. 191.

56 ibid., p. 190.

57 H. Kelsen, 'Wesen und Entwicklung der Staatsgerichtsbarkeit' in H. Triepel, M. Layer, and E. von Hippel (eds), *Verhandlungen der Tagung der Deutschen Staatsrechtslehrer zu Wien am 23. Und 24 April 1928* (Negotiations of the Conference on German Constitutional Law at Vienna on 23 and 24 April 1928), 1929, pp. 30–84.

58 Cf. M. Troper, 'Kelsen et le contrôle de constitutionnalité', C.-M. Herrera (ed.), *Le Droit, le*

that are enacted by the legislature, but also on administrative acts. The former are examined in relation to the Constitution, the latter in relation to the laws.

Kelsen's reply to this first objection, an objection that gave precedence to the sovereignty of parliament over the constitutional court, was connected with a 'hierarchical' concept of the legal order. In fact this is the meaning of his theory of the formation of law by levels ('Stufenbau der Normen'). In this theory, the legal order is seen as a single chain starting with the constitution, running on to judicial rulings, with no qualitative differences arising among the different levels. All levels of the legal order belong to a unitary system,[59] its coherence acting as its leavening. The constitution (constitutional law), laws, regulations, judgements and administrative decisions belong to a hierarchy of rules, in which the creation of each is 'determined by a still higher norm.'[60] This hierarchy of the legal order guarantees that the constitution regulates and determines the whole public order.[61] For Kelsen,

> The legal order [...] is therefore not a system of norms coordinated to each other, standing, so to speak, side by side on the same level, but a hierarchy of different levels of norms. The unity of these norms is constituted by the fact that the creation of one norm – the lower one – is determined by another – the higher – the creation of which is determined by a still higher norm, and that this *regressus* is terminated by a highest, the basic norm which, being the supreme reason of validity of the whole legal order, constitutes its unity. [62]

The legal nature of each norm depends on its insertion into this very complex hierarchy, the cohesion of which is also guaranteed by the constitutional court. Finally, the coherence of the legal order is secured only if the constitution is binding in this hierarchical order, i.e. only if 'quashing unconstitutional actions'[63] is made possible by a constitutional court.

However, such a hierarchy in the order does not imply that all of its levels are strictly determined by one another. A lower norm, of whatever kind – legislation, administrative decision, judicial ruling – is never derived completely from a higher norm. At each stage of the hierarchy of the legal order, a decision is required, and 'the higher norm is always an empowering norm.'[64] As Stanley Paulson says, 'the

politique autour de Max Weber, Carl Schmitt, Paris: L'Harmattan, 1995, p. 171.

59 This aspect is noted by F. Weyr, 'La "Stufentheorie" de la théorie pure du droit vue par un Français', (1934), *Revue internationale de la théorie du droit*, année VIII, 1966, p. 235.

60 H. Kelsen, *General Theory of Law and State*, p. 124.

61 H. Kelsen, 'Wesen und Entwicklung...', p. 35.

62 H. Kelsen, *General Theory of Law and State*, p. 124.

63 H. Kelsen, 'Wesen und Entwicklung...', p. 78.

64 S. L. Paulson, 'Arguments "conceptuels" de Schmitt à l'encontre du contrôle de constitutionnalité et réponses de Kelsen. Un aspect de l'affrontement entre Schmitt et Kelsen sur le "gardien de la

result of this dynamic concept [of the Stufenbau] is a relativisation of the differences between creating law and applying it, and therefore in a way a relativisation of the status of the different kinds of law themselves.'[65] This 'dynamic' concept, made possible by taking into account the decisional dimension at each level, allows on the one hand, a response to the critics who reproach the Kelsenian hierarchy of the legal order for excessive rigidity, and on the other hand, the signifying, in another way, the unity of that hierarchy.

In the second objection that confronted Kelsen, the constitutional court was seen as a violation of the principle of the separation of powers.[66] To this, Kelsen replied that in a democracy the separation of powers implies a reciprocal monitoring of the bodies of the state by one another.

> This is not only to prevent the concentration of excessive power in the hands of a single body – which would be dangerous to democracy – but also to guarantee the regularity of the operation of the various bodies. So not only is the institution of a constitutional court not in contradiction with the separation of powers, it is in fact an affirmation of it.[67]

In 1928, Kelsen opposed this objection to the violation of the separation of powers by putting into perspective the difference in kind between the legislative and the judicial functions (as he was to enlarge upon in *Wer soll der Hüter der Verfassung sein?* [*Who Should Be the Guardian of the Constitution?*] in 1931).[68] When a constitutional court repeals a law, in a way it is exercising a legislative function: 'a court that has the power to repeal laws is thereby an institution of the legislative power.'[69] This is the very definition of a negative legislator.[70]

---

constitution"', in C.-M. Herrera (ed.), *Le Droit, le politique autour de Max Weber, Carl Schmitt,* Paris: L'Harmattan, 1995, p. 255.

65 ibid., p. 256.

66 This is also Schmitt's criticism. Schmitt thought that assigning to the judiciary the role of guardian of the constitution, violated the rule of the separation of powers, since issues relating to the preservation of the constitution are political, not judicial. Cf. Carl Schmitt, *Der Hüter der Verfassung,* (1931), Berlin: Duncker & Humblot, 1996, p. 36.

67 H. Kelsen, 'Wesen und Entwicklung...', p. 55.

68 H. Kelsen, *Wer soll der Hüter der Verfassung sein?* [*Who Should Be the Guardian of the Constitution?*] Berlin: W. Rothschild, 1931.

69 H. Kelsen, 'Wesen und Entwicklung...', p. 55.

70 'If a "court" has the power to repeal a law, then it is authorized to establish a general norm, because the repeal of a law has the same general character as the enactment of a law. So repealing laws is actually a legislative function, and a court repealing a law is a body with legislative power.' H. Kelsen, *Wer soll der Hüter...,* p. 27, note 1.

In the interwar years, Kelsen was to have many opportunities to revisit the justifications for the constitutional court. He was to do so brilliantly in the quarrel that set him in opposition to Schmitt. This polemic, emblematic of their confrontation, culminated in two successive publications, the second of which was a scathing reply that Kelsen addressed to Schmitt. In 1931, the same year that Schmitt's *Der Hüter der Verfassung* (*The Guardian of the Constitution*) appeared, Kelsen replied with *Wer soll der Hüter der Verfassung sein?* (*Who Should Be the Guardian of the Constitution?*). In this essay, Kelsen defended the legitimacy of a constitutional court by combating the reasons that Schmitt cites for assigning the role of guardian of the Constitution to the President of the Reich. The dispute between these two lawyers was about which body of the state should be assigned the role of guardian of the German Constitution. Kelsen thought this mission ought to be conferred on the judiciary, especially the Constitutional Court, while Schmitt thought the task should be given to the top of the executive, the President of the Reich. While for Kelsen, 'guarding' the Constitution required the establishment of constitutional review, for Schmitt, this guarantee was to be achieved by strengthening the powers of the President of the Reich, and especially by clearly defining that office and making it independent. To Schmitt, fulfilling the President's role as guardian of the Constitution meant preserving public order, and, whenever in the President's eyes the situation required, proclaiming a state of emergency and resorting to government by decree.

To appreciate the full meaning of this controversy, we should see it as part of two debates of a very different kind that go far beyond the polemics that these two lawyers engaged in, and that explain the attention that Schmitt gave to the presidential office, and Kelsen to the constitutional court. In the first place, Kelsen's reflections are part of the project to overhaul the institutions of constitutional law, some results of which can be seen in Austria, but also in postwar Germany. Usually we see the arrival of the 'European model of constitutional law' in the Constitution of the new Austrian Federal Republic on the 1st of October 1920, in its legal body which was responsible for deciding questions of constitutionality by a 'centralised monitoring of the constitutionality of laws.'[71] This central and specialised kind of monitoring, theoretically developed by Kelsen, was to especially inspire Spain, Italy, France and the Federal Republic of Germany.[72]

---

71 A. Le Divellec, 'Les prémices de la justice constitutionnelle en Allemagne avant 1945', in D. Chagnollaud, *Aux origines du contrôle de constitutionnalité XVIIIe-XXe siècle*, Paris: LGDJ, 2000, p. 130. Cf. Article 89 of the Austrian Federal Constitution ('Österreichische Bundesverfassung') of 1 October 1920.

72 The European model of constitutional courts, paternity of which can be attributed to Kelsen, is generally contrasted to the American model, in which 'constitutional justice is entrusted to the whole judicial apparatus, and [...] in fact is not distinguished from ordinary justice, in that disputes, regardless of their nature, are judged by the same courts and in substantially the same conditions'. L. Favoreu, *Les Cours constitutionnelles*, 2nd ed., Paris: PUF, 1992, p. 5.

As Armel Le Divellec emphasises, the model of constitutional law, as envisaged in the Austrian Constitution, had appeared chronologically first, or at any rate simultaneously, in some German Länder in the Weimar Republic.[73] However, the option chosen in the Weimar Constitution was less bold than the one introduced by Austria in 1920, because it did not envisage a central body to review constitutional law, and a multiplicity of authorities undertook this task. Dissatisfaction with this multitude and this imbroglio of decision-making bodies acting as 'guarantors of the Constitution', led in Weimar, to the emergence of projects for a true constitutional court, including those of Heinrich Triepel in 1924 and Gerhard Anschütz in 1926.[74] But these were not to be realised. The Kelsenian contributions toward a constitutional court were part of these reflections and projects.

In the second place, the attention that Schmitt gave to the presidency, which he named the guardian of the Constitution, can be seen as a continuation of the constitutional deliberations of the Weimar National Assembly, which ended when the Constitution came into force in August 1919. One part of the heated debate that had enlivened that Assembly, was to do with the role and the prerogatives of the President of the Reich. As recalled by Wolfgang Mommsen,[75] this controversy basically opposed the supporters of a plebiscitary leader (the Democratic Party) to the Social Democrats, at that time the majority who wanted to reduce the President's prerogatives as much as possible. Conversely, the Democratic Party, supported by the right-wing parties, did not want the President to be merely 'a representative figure'.[76] In this controversy, which spread beyond the work of the Assembly, Schmitt took up with those in favour of upgrading the presidential office, including this in his *Der Hüter der Verfassung*. That work was also in perfect harmony with a presidentialisation of the Weimar regime in 1930, very popular with conservatives.[77] Thus, this controversy about the guardian of the Constitution that set Schmitt against Kelsen is at the confluence of two very different debates and of two conflicting doctrinal universes, widely mobilised in this *disputatio*. This makes even more prominent, Kelsen's legal-political concern for the compliance of actions by the state with the Constitution, the ultimate source of the balance of power in a democracy.

---

73 A. Le Divellec, 'Les prémices de la justice...', p. 130.

74 Cf. J.-C. Béguin, *Le Contrôle de la constitutionnalité des lois en République fédérale d'Allemagne*, Paris: Economica, 1982, p. 20.

75 W. Mommsen *et al.*, *Max Weber et la politique allemande (1890–1920)*, especially 'Destin ultérieur des exigences constitutionnelles de Max Weber', Paris: Presses universitaires de France, 1985 pp. 465–477.

76 ibid., p. 471. Cf. J. Van Tichelen, *Le Président de la République et le problème de l'État*, Paris: Alcan, 1939, especially pp. 83–85.

77 This policy shift took the form of the system known as 'presidential cabinets', governing by emergency orders (Article 48) signed by the President, and by repeated dissolutions of the Reichstag.

According to Kelsen, constitutional law plays another important role in the preservation of balances, this time not between different institutions of the state, but in the relations that get established between majorities and minorities. Finding a different way to counter the arguments that oppose a constitutional court by claiming it is antidemocratic, Kelsen draws the rationale for such a court from his reflections on protecting minorities.[78] Constitutional law acts as a shield for minorities whose rights could be violated by 'despotic' majorities:

> Thus the minority must have the possibility of direct or indirect recourse to the constitutional court, if we want to guarantee the minority's meaningful political existence and effectiveness, both so essential for democracy; if we do not want to expose it to the arbitrariness of the majority; and if we want the Constitution to be more than a *lex imperfecta*.[79]

The controversy between Schmitt and Kelsen over the guarantee of the Constitution ascended to a general reflection on the balance of power and the checking mechanisms used in democratic regimes. For Kelsen, the fate of democracy is closely bound up with its checking procedures and with its capacity to respect the principle of legality. Without these it is in danger of collapsing.

---

78 The threat to the majority of an appeal to a constitutional court acts to protect the minority: H. Kelsen, 'Wesen und Entwicklung...', p. 81.

79 H. Kelsen, *Vom Wesen und Wert...*, p. 209.

chapter three | controversy over the relationship between law and the state

The Legal Order as the Ultimate Source of Cohesion

Kelsen's democratic theory is inseparable from his reflections on the sources of the unity of the state.[1] What is it in a democratic regime that makes for the state's cohesion? Is it sociological, political or legal? In the period after the First World War, a number of jurists, in addition to Kelsen, were raising this question. It is a question at a high level of generality about the sustainability of the state in a democratic system. In this controversy over the origins of political unity, in which, among others, the advocates of positivism and anti-positivism squared off against each other, Kelsen bluntly asserts that the unity of the state lies in submission to a common social order, as this order emerges in legislative deliberations. In his view, the people appear as a people in a reasonably accurate way only from the legal point of view; the 'unity of the people is basically just a legal fact: the unity of behaviour of the people subject to the norms regulating the governmental legal order'.[2] Kelsen's assertion is expressed in his definition of the state:

> [T]he state is a specific normative unit, not a structure that can somehow be understood in terms of causal laws. It is the legal order; as a super-individual will, it is the personification of the legal order. So the standard dualism of state and law constitutes an unacceptable doubling of legal-normative subject matter.[3]

---

1   Thus, Kelsen began his article 'The conception of the state and social psychology: with special reference to Freud's group theory', (*International Journal of Psycho-Analysis*, 1924, vol. 5) p. 1 (written in 1921) with this question: 'in what manner, according to what criterion, is this multitude of individuals welded into what we are wont to assume to be a higher unity? [...] How do the separate individuals forming the state, or their individual activities, combine into a super-individual whole? [...] This inquiry is, however, also identical with that concerning the peculiar "reality" of the state, the specific nature of its being'.

2   H. Kelsen, *Vom Wesen und Wert der Demokratie*, 1929, in M. Jestaedt and O. Lepsius (eds) *Verteidigung der Demokratie*, Tübingen: Mohr Siebeck, 2006, p. 163.

3   H. Kelsen, Preface to the second (unchanged) edition of *Der soziologische und der juristische Staatsbegriff: Kritische Untersuchung des Verhältnisses zwischen Staat und Recht* (1922), Aalen: Scientia Verlag, 1962, page v.

Kelsen treats attempts to base the unity of the state on sociological-political reflections as fictitious. In the *General Theory of Law and State*, he goes through the doctrines that anchor the unity of the state in a sociological foundation but, according to him, actually pursue objectives that are not primarily descriptive; in fact they conceal ideological aims. Kelsen describes these doctrinal alternatives in order to emphasise their limitations and false assumptions. Four types of doctrines in particular are questioned here, and all of them are elements that he 'purifies' out of his doctrine of the state:

First, *interactionist theories* base the unity of the state on the intensity of interactions, seeing a greater density of interactions among members of the same state than among individuals who do not belong to the same political community. This approach was inspired especially by the work of Georg Simmel (1858–1918), for whom a society is formed only if individuals interact.[4] To Kelsen, this is political fiction, not really based on observations. The density of interactions can be stronger among individuals not belonging to the same state; for example, among inhabitants of border regions.

Secondly, theories that erect social unity on the *general will* or the *common interest* postulate a convergence of will among members of the same community. According to Kelsen, these doctrines – an eloquent illustration of which is found in Rousseau – are essentially used to deny the conflicts that can arise in a state, and are therefore, by nature, ideological. Moreover, granting a certain reality to the concept of the 'will of the state' 'is to hypostatise[5] an abstraction into a real agency, that is, to ascribe to a normative relation between individuals a substantial or personal character'.[6] To Kelsen, this process characterises certain tendencies in political thought in which a real entity replaces an abstraction. In many cases, it gets back to the idea of a state will, to which one must not attribute a supra-empirical or mystical character; such a will is rather the expression of a legal order.[7] The will of the state is only the product of a prescriptive system that imposes onto wills and actions a degree of conformity. For Kelsen, to hypostatise the state, or its will, is a process that is characteristic of primitive thought.[8]

---

4   Cf. H. Kelsen, 'The conception of the state and social psychology...', p. 2.

5   By 'hypostatise', is meant, to change one category into another, in this instance an abstraction into a real entity.

6   H. Kelsen, *General Theory of Law and State*, trans. A. Wedberg, Cambridge, Mass.: Harvard University Press, 1945, p. 185.

7   'After all, this "will" of the state (and the state itself) is only an anthropomorphic expression of the unity of an order....' H. Kelsen, *Der soziologische und der juristische Staatsbegriff*, p. 69.

8   H. Kelsen, *General Theory of Law and State*, p. 185. In 'The conception of the state and social psychology...', pp. 36–37, Kelsen discusses the tendency of primitive thought to hypostasis, which still deeply permeates the social and legal sciences: 'it seems merely a difference of degree if natural science presupposes "forces" behind phenomena where primitives still imagine gods. In principle therefore it is the same thing when for primitive totemistic thought, social unity, the

Thirdly, *organic theories* understand the state as in some sense a natural or social organism in which the whole is greater than the sum of the parts. This perspective can be best understood by paying attention to its biological analogy: the state is likened to an organism, each attribute of which relates to a function. The common feature of organic theories, as expressed in the theories of Otto von Gierke (1841–1921) and Oscar Hertwig (1849–1922), is their refusal to explain social formations – particularly states – in terms of their primary atoms, in this case individuals. Organic theories understand the state as if it were a natural or social organism, the whole of which transcends the sum of the parts. According to Kelsen, these theories are an example of a hypostasis i.e. of a fiction that encourages obedience. Likening the state to an organism contains a self-legitimising component, since nothing can be subtracted or added without distorting it.

Fourthly, the doctrine that views the state as a *power of domination* between governors and governed, illustrated in Max Weber's thinking, constitutes, in Kelsen's opinion, the most successful sociological theory of the state, which nevertheless remains questionable in its presuppositions:

> There is, as a matter of fact, no State where all commands 'in the name of the State' originate in one single ruler. There are always more than one commanding authority, and always a large number of factual relations of domination, numerous acts of commanding and obeying, the sum of which represents the 'sociological State'.[9]

Theories seeing the foundation of the state in monolithic domination ignore the multiplicity of relations of domination, which according to Kelsen converge only because of the legal order to which they are subjected.

Against sociological or indeed psychological doctrines of political unity, Kelsen opposed the fact of plurality, and asserted that unity was not to be found in social reality, and could come only from the legal sphere. All that is social is necessarily divided, not convergent. For Kelsen this plurality remains unshrinkable. He systematically dismisses from legal and political reflections all fictions and myths, including those of political unity, because they distort debates

---

combining of a multitude of individuals into a unity, can only be expressed in the visible and palpable substance of the sacrificial (totem) animal devoured in common, and when modern politics and law can only conceive of this abstract social code, this system of legal and compelling norms, the unity that is to say of the limiting social community (and the community consists solely in this code), as something of the nature of a substance, as a "real", entirely anthropomorphically constructed "person", without becoming aware of the peculiar character of this idea as merely a makeshift for thought, especially when it is observed how strong the tendency is to elevate this "person" somehow into a visible and tangible something, into a supra-biological creature. If modern politics is primitive in this respect, the totemic system is just the politics of primitives'.

9   H. Kelsen, *General Theory of Law and State*, p. 187.

and uselessly burden them with an ideological aura. The political community always remains legal, not empirical-causal.[10]

What is at Stake in the Analogy between Theology and Theory of the State

In Kelsen's view, all theories that try to see the democratic state and its unity otherwise than by looking at the legal order that it personifies are futile because they cannot achieve their purpose. His reflections about the sources of political unity are part of a comprehensive effort to expose the weakness of all doctrines that seek to found the state on a sociological basis, which on examination turns out to be without foundation, in his view. This exposure coincides with his fight against dualistic doctrines that reject the unity (or identity) of law and the state. In a rather unexpected way, Kelsen, in order to condemn non-monistic doctrines definitively, has recourse to an analogy between the (dualistic) doctrine of the state and theology. This comparison occupies a significant place in Kelsen's interwar works and in his autobiographical letter of 1927.[11] The main places where he sketches this analogy are in 'Ueber Staatsunrecht' (1913)[12], 'The conception of the state and social psychology' (1922), 'Gott und Staat' (1922–1923), 'Der soziologische und der juristische Staatsbegriff' (1922), and *Allgemeine Staatslehre* (1925).[13] Kelsen deploys this analogy far removed from theological issues, ultimately using analogies he establishes between theology and doctrines about the state, only to demonstrate the dangers of an understanding of the state that transcends law and is autonomous from the legal sphere. For Kelsen, in the problems they face and the solutions they provide, theology and the theory of the state have a troubling affinity:

> The perfect parallelism between the logical structure of the state and the concepts of God shows up in the extraordinary similarity of problems and solutions to problems in the theory of the state and in theology. Theology's main problem – the relationship between God and the universe (or between God and nature) – perfectly matches the core question posed by the theory of the state, namely the relationship between state and law.[14]

---

10 H. Kelsen, 'The conception of the state and social psychology...', p. 3.

11 Cf. H. Kelsen, 'Selsbstdarstellung', (1927), in M. Jestaedt (ed.), *Hans Kelsen im Selbstzeugnis*, Tübingen: Mohr Siebeck, 2006, pp. 21–29 at pp. 25–26.

12 Cf. H. Kelsen, *Der soziologische und der juristische Staatsbegriff*, pp. 220–222.

13 Full references of Kelsen's works can be found in the Select Bibliography of Kelsen's Writings.

14 H. Kelsen, *Der soziologische und der juristische Staatsbegriff*, p. 222. This argument is developed in the chapter 'Staat und Recht: Gott und Natur'.

All of Kelsen's reflections in these texts of 1913, 1922 and 1925 conclude that a clear distinction between the sphere of law and that of the state is not warranted. How does he go about exploiting this analogy between theology and doctrines about the state to reaffirm his opposition to dualistic theories?

For Kelsen, God and the state, each in their manner, represent a personification of two abstract ideas. The order of the world finds concrete expression in the shape of God. Similarly, the state can be envisaged as a personified legal order or a legal person. It is the 'personification' of the legal system that makes possible the process of imputation by which an action is imputed to the state, if and only if the state is determined by the normative system. The diversity of legal relations among individuals falls under the political sphere only if the state personifies the legal order, i.e. only if it implements it.[15] Kelsen is not opposed to personifications as such, which are very useful for explaining a phenomenon, but he does reject personifications that become hypostases. While a personification remains a means of knowing, a metaphor that makes an abstract idea more intelligible, a hypostasis on the other hand, no longer acts as a metaphor, but presupposes this idea really, concretely exists. For Kelsen, to hypostasise the state assumes that it is regarded as an entity in itself, independently of, or previously to, the legal order. As in other contexts, he emphasises the dangers of a hypostasised state, made autonomous from law and from individuals.

Just as theology can exist only insofar as it differs from the moral and natural sciences, and sees a transcendent, supernatural God, so the dualist theory of the state – as opposed to the monistic[16] theory – is possible only if one presupposes a state that transcends law, and if one admits the idea of a super-legal state. Kelsen cleverly compares dualistic doctrines to animist superstitions that attribute a soul to natural phenomena. By analogy, supporters of dualistic doctrines imagine that at the source of the law there is a spirit, in this case a hypostasised state:

---

15 'The problem of the State is a problem of imputation. The State is, so to speak, a common point into which various human actions are projected, a common point of imputation for different human actions. The individuals whose actions are considered to be acts of the State, whose actions are imputed to the State, are designated as "organs" of the State and only some actions by those capable are acts of the State. What is the criterion of this imputation? This is the decisive question leading to the essence of the State. An analysis shows that we impute a human action to the State only when the human action in question corresponds in a specific way to the presupposed legal order. The imputation of a human action to the State is possible only on the condition that this action is determined in a specific way by a normative order; and this order is the legal order'. H. Kelsen, *General Theory of Law and State*, pp. 191–192.

16 The term 'monistic' refers to doctrines saying that the state cannot be distinguished from the legal order.

The dualism of law and State is a superfluous doubling or duplication of the object of our cognition; a result of our tendency to personify and then to hypostatise our personifications. A typical example of this tendency is found in the animistic interpretation of nature, that is, primitive man's idea that nature is animated, that behind everything there is a soul, a spirit, a god of this thing: behind a tree, a dryad, behind a river, a nymph, behind the moon, a moon-goddess, behind the sun, a sun-god. Thus, we imagine behind the law, its hypostatised personification, the State, the god of the law. The dualism of law and state is an animistic superstition.[17]

In Kelsen's account, intervention by God in the laws of nature and by the state in the legal order are similarly conceived and treated. These issues are resolved by theology, as by the dualist theory of the state, by using the concept of the 'miraculous'. Theology recognises that the world is governed by the laws of nature. But it cannot similarly admit that God is also subject to them. For Kelsen, theology guarantees God's freedom with respect to nature by the idea of the miracle, which is nothing other than the worldly manifestation of actions emanating from the will of a superhuman power. In miracles, God withdraws from the natural laws, but without denying the rules that govern nature. So how does this work in terms of the theory of the state? Kelsen introduces the idea of the 'legal miracle' to describe situations in which the theory of the state makes intelligible what would otherwise be inconceivable from this viewpoint. Even though this is not explicitly mentioned, it is likely that Kelsen is thinking about everything that does not follow from the hierarchy of the legal order, about what is legally unintelligible. If the acts coming from the state, but not strictly falling within the legal order are not considered to be illegal, that demonstrates for Kelsen, that we are in the presence of a 'legal miracle': we have exited legality – metaphorically, the laws of nature – but it is not deemed to be illegal. Kelsenian normativism remaining hostile to anything that bursts in on the legal order, the expression 'legal miracle' is derogatory and does not in any way legitimate emancipation from that order. Any extra-legal, heteronomous intervention clashes both with Kelsen's legal positivism and with his conception of democracy.

Building on the analogies that he had made, Kelsen established a relationship between theodicy – the presupposition of a good God, even taking into account the existence of evil in the world – and the assumption of a 'just' or legitimate state, in spite of illegal practices, which metaphorically represent evil in the legal/state order. Theodicy, transposed into the domain of the state, means that the state retains its legitimacy, even if it has recourse to practices that are neither defined nor anticipated by the legal order. For Kelsen, this entails as a pernicious result, the impossibility of calling a state's actions illegal, even if they are demonstrably not in accordance with the positive laws. This corresponds metaphorically to the

---

17 H. Kelsen, *General Theory of Law and State*, p. 191.

infallibility of the Pope, the Church's representative on Earth. With these various transpositions, Kelsen exposes the processes that allow, or even encourage, the state to become independent of the legal setting, and which thus give it a kind of immunity or freedom in respect to the legal order. The dualism of state and law is an improper political-legal idea that allows the misuse of political principles contradictory to positive law. According to Kelsen, the state organises its state activity in such a way that the legal and state spheres cannot be separated from each other. That is the primary implication of his monistic doctrine of the state. In this perspective, the origin of the state can only be normative, which by definition excludes sociological roots. A sociological unity can arise out of the legal order that shapes and coordinates individuals' behaviour, but not vice versa.

According to Kelsen, the theory of the state and theology confront each other in similar problems if they postulate transcendence, meaning either God's autonomy from the world or the state's from law. In theology, the idea of a transcendent God implies that God's nature is radically different from men's, otherwise he is not transcendent. However, for God to maintain a positive relationship with the world and men, it is necessary that God and the world share some common elements – which would be contradictory with the postulate that God's nature is different from men's. So how can the transcendence of God and his heterogeneity in relation to the world be reconciled with his 'harmonious' relationship with the world? For Kelsen, theology resolves this contradiction by turning to the miracle of the incarnation of God on Earth. This has 'legal' implications because it assumes a kind of self-limitation of God through the person of Christ.[18] This argument is of interest only in its application to the state-legal sphere. Comparing that sphere with theology, what is the problem that confronts the state? If we consider the state's sphere as above the law, i.e. that it transcends the law, then it is impossible to understand the non-contradictory relation between law and the state. How can the independence of the state in a dualist perspective be reconciled with its status of representative of the legal order? For dualistic theorists there remains an alternative to monistic doctrines: the theory of the self-limitation of the state. Georg Jellinek is an eminent representative of this theory, which allows one to avoid reducing the state to a legal entity, and also to explain the positive (non-contradictory) relationship between law and the state. The self-limitation of the sphere of the state presupposes that the state, as a sovereign power, by the limits that it imposes on itself, becomes a rule-of-law state.[19] According to Kelsen,

---

18 'This theory of God's incarnation in the world is put forward in theology under the aspect of the self-limitation and self-obligation of God'. H. Kelsen, 'God and the State', (1922–1923), in O. Weinberger (ed. and intro.), *Hans Kelsen: Essays in Legal and Moral Philosophy*, trans. P. Heath, Dordrecht (Netherlands) and Boston (USA): D. Reidel Publishing Company, 1973, p. 73.

19 Here I am adopting Léon Duguit's definition of 'the self-limited state' (*'l'État autolimité'*): 'by voluntarily accepting the obligations of a legal rule that it (the state) has made itself or by a contract it has made, it submits to the law, it limits its action by the law; it is legally bound. But in

the theory of self-limitation joins up with dualistic doctrines, and yields to the temptation of a hypostasised state; therefore he rejects it. For him, only monistic doctrines – those that identify the state with law – manage to resolve satisfactorily the relationship between law and the state. Any other perspective leaves this issue unresolved, as is clear in the *General Theory of Law and State* (1945):

> The problem of the so-called auto-obligation of the State is one of those pseudo-problems that result from the erroneous dualism of State and law. This dualism is, in turn, due to a fallacy of which we meet numerous examples in the history of all fields of human thought. Our desire for the intuitive representation of abstractions leads us to personify the unity of a system, and then to hypostasise the personification. What originally was only a way of representing the unity of a system of objects becomes a new object, existing in its own right.[20]

Theories of self-limitation, such as Georg Jellinek's, inspired other opposition, including that of the French publicist Léon Duguit, which would be equalled only by Kelsen's.[21] In his *Traité de droit constitutionnel* (*Treaty of Constitutional Law*, 1911), Duguit exposed the sophistic character of theories that involve a self-limitation that conceals the omnipotence of the state:

> self-limitation theory contains some real sleight of hand. Voluntary subordination is not subordination. The state is not really limited by the law if the state alone can introduce and write this law, and if it can at any time make any changes that it wants to make in it. This kind of foundation of public law is clearly extremely fragile.[22]

As long as the state is bound up with public law by its own will, it retains its omnipotence. The sovereignty of the state and limitations on exercising its power – differently stated, the sovereign power of the state and obeying rules of public law – cannot be reconciled: 'either the state is sovereign, and therefore, always deciding by its own will, it cannot be subject to mandatory rules that limit it; or

---

spite of that, its sovereign *Herrschaft* remains intact, because its will to submit to law – to laws, to contracts – has been determined only by itself. The modern state is therefore a *Rechtsstaat*, a rule-of-law state'. L. Duguit, 'La doctrine allemande de l'autolimitation de l'État', *Revue de droit public*, vol. XXVI, 1919, p. 167.

20 H. Kelsen, *General Theory of Law and State,* p. 198.

21 In 1926, together with Franz Weyr and Léon Duguit, Kelsen founded the *Revue internationale de la théorie du droit.*

22 L. Duguit, *Traité de droit constitutionnel,* vol. I, *La règle du droit: le problème de l'État,* Paris: de Boccard, 1911, p. 645.

it is subject to such rules, and therefore is not sovereign'.[23] Like Duguit, Kelsen emphasised the difficulties and contradictions inherent in the theory of self-limitation. Reconciling the omnipotence of the state with its subjection to law turns out to be a perilous or even a sophistic exercise. But if Kelsen rejects the compromise solution of self-limitation, what meaning does he give to state sovereignty in a democratic order? If meaning resides exclusively in the validity of a system of norms and in the expression of the unity of an order,[24] then sovereignty boils down to a process of imputation, i.e. it 'restricts' itself to the application and implementation of a legal order. That is a definition of sovereignty that has sometimes been understood as an attempt to get rid of the concept itself, as Otto Kirchheimer (1905–1965) asserts.[25]

While the Kelsenian analogy between theology and the theory of the state was intended to update and to challenge the assumptions of dualistic doctrines, this comparison is also pursued with a view to countering the political theology of Carl Schmitt. Using ecclesiastical institutions as a model for thinking about the state is the bedrock of Schmittian political theology. One of the major things at stake here is Schmitt's reformulation of the definition of representation, to restore in a republican context 'transcendence' and the custom of emergency powers: to him, the infallibility of the Pope in the spiritual order equates to sovereignty in the political order. To Kelsen, Schmittian political theology is just an elaborate form of dualism: the state, especially through its emergency powers, is authorised to side-step the legal order. Moreover, according to Schmitt, sovereignty is defined and is expressed outside of the legality of ordinary times. The confrontation between these two jurists culminates in their very different views of the relationship between the political and legal spheres. While Schmitt never tires of distinguishing between them, in that way making the image of the sovereign emerge, Kelsen asserts their unity or their identity and thus puts sovereignty back within the limits of enforcing the law. In 1922 Kelsen recognised his debt to the analysis of Sigmund Freud, who had related hypostases of society, of the state and of God to individual psychology, and had thus uncovered these mechanisms and their primitive origins,[26] which in his view the sciences (including legal science) ought to dispense with. For Kelsen, Schmittian political theology was merely one illustration of this tendency to hypostasis and to the mythification of the state.

---

23 ibid., p. 632.

24 A. J. Merkl, 'Rezension von: Hans Kelsen, *Allgemeine Staatslehre*, Berlin 1925', (1926), in D. Mayer-Maly, H. Schambeck, and W. D. Grussmann, (eds) *Gesammelte Schriften*, Berlin: Duncker & Humblot, 1995, p. 70.

25 O. Kirchheimer, 'Remarques sur la théorie de la souveraineté nationale en Allemagne et en France', *Archives de philosophie du droit et de sociologie juridique*, 1934, vol. 1–2, pp. 250–251.

26 H. Kelsen, 'The conception of the state and social psychology...'.

chapter four | conclusion: hans kelsen in our time[1]

Hans Kelsen's reflections on democracy converge on a quest for the criteria that distinguish this form of government from other systems of political organisation. In his view, democracy's distinctiveness comes from its respect for the principle of self-determination: norms are worked out through the autonomy of the will of the members of the state or their representatives. From this basic distinctive criterion of autonomy comes the other characteristics that Kelsen describes throughout his work. Relativism has a central role in his democratic theory. Political liberty or autonomy is not compatible with a metaphysical understanding of the world. Kelsen emphasises, in several ways, how the assertion of absolute values is contradictory to democratic theory. He also shows how natural law is exposed to the same difficulties when it tries to make its premises compatible with respect for democratic rules.[2]

For Kelsen, the principle of self-determination is incompatible with any obedience to norms or values that are not debatable and negotiable. 'For that is the big question: whether there is knowledge of absolute truth, an insight into absolute values.'[3] According to Kelsen, the answer given to this question is what distinguishes democratic regimes from autocratic regimes: the former reply in the negative and the latter reply in the affirmative. This relativism means so much to Kelsen that it extends to political leaders as well as to governing majorities. Leaders occupy positions of power not because they are the best, but because they have been appointed to govern. In 1925, Kelsen explicitly opposed this positivist, relativist characterisation of majorities, and of political leaders, to fascism[4] and to all forms of autocracy. As he sees it, while democracy is relativistic, it must therefore be critical. In contrast to autocratic regimes, rulers are responsible and accountable for their actions. In a striking phrase, Kelsen (in 'State-Form and World-Outlook', 1933) remarked that democracy's 'scientific strength' is its 'political weakness'.[5] Exposed to rationalisation, lacking strong ideological protection, democracy is subject to a constant demand for justification.

---

1 Revised and enlarged for the English edition.

2 Kelsen's definition of democracy, focused as it is on the principle of self-government, does introduce some limitations into Kelsen's thinking; we shall come back to these later in this concluding chapter.

3 H. Kelsen, *Vom Wesen und Wert der Demokratie*, Tübingen, J.C.B. Mohr, 1929, republished in H. Kelsen, *Verteidigung der Demokratie*, (eds) M. Jestaedt and O. Lepsius, Tübingen: Mohr Siebeck, 2006, p. 224.

4 H. Kelsen, *Das Problem des Parlamentarismus*, Wein: Wilhelm Braumüller, 1925, pp. 41–42, n. 18.

5 H. Kelsen, 'State-form and world-outlook', [1933] in O. Weinberger (ed.) trans. P. Heath, *Hans Kelsen: Essays in Legal and Moral Philosophy*, Boston: D. Reidel Publishing, 1973, p. 109.

In what follows I want to develop two things mentioned above that demonstrate the vibrant topicality of Kelsen's political thought: first, the principle of self-determination (or self-government) and the limits that can be legitimately imposed on it; and secondly, possible ways of increasing rulers' responsibility to the ruled.

The Limits of Self-Government

We have already noticed the importance that Kelsen gives to self-determination as a specific feature of democracy: people live in a democracy insofar as they abide by rules that they have chosen. But even though autonomy is the distinguishing characteristic of democracy, and it underlies the opposition between democracy and autocracy, Kelsen ponders and theorises the limits of self-government. And this is one of the parts of his work that resonates most with political theorists in our time, as Adam Przeworski noticed in relation to his own work.[6] The limitations on self-government proposed by Kelsen are set out in order to defend a particular conception of democracy, namely constitutional parliamentary democracy. Kelsen limits the principle of self-government for basically two kinds of reason.

First, there is its impracticality. The size of modern states and the impossibility of reaching a consensus makes it necessary to have delegation, i.e. representative government. Consequently not all citizens are included in the whole political decision making process, but only in the choice of their representatives. In addition, the rule of self-determination – which means that the social order will be created by the unanimous decision of all the subjects and that this order remains valid only as long as it inspires the confidence of everyone – proves to be impractical. Therefore the irreducible divergence of interests and values makes majority rule necessary in democracies. These reasons for limiting self-government, which are theorised and defended by Kelsen, are still generally accepted in the literature. In established democracies, majority decisions and the principle of delegation by representatives are taken for granted, even though they are, as we shall see below, accompanied by correctives.

Secondly, these very limits, that life in modern states imposes on the principle of self-government, themselves generate dangers that Kelsen was perfectly aware of and which imply further limitations on the democratic decision making process. This second aspect is clearly more controversial. For Kelsen, the unlimited practice of majority decision making is perilous, because of the risk of tyranny that it imposes on individuals in the minority. This peril – identified well before Kelsen, by writers such as James Madison, Benjamin Constant, Alexis de Tocqueville and John Stuart Mill – remains at the heart of debate about democracy today: to what extent should majority decisions be submitted to safeguards?

---

6 In his article on 'Self-government in our time', *Annual Review of Political Science*, 2009, vol. 12, pp. 71–92, Prezworski frequently cites Kelsen.

Moderation by Reviewing Constitutionality

If Kelsen is right that the devices that moderate majority decisions cannot be found in a natural order, or in any metaphysics whatsoever, where do legitimate limits on the majority principle reside? According to him, these limits are both legal and political. Let us start with the former. For Kelsen, devices that moderate majority decisions reside first of all in a constitutional court. Kelsen here continues the doctrine of the school that theorised the conditions of an effective guarantee of the constitutional order, later perpetuated by proponents of constitutional democracy such as Ronald Dworkin. The spectre of despotism of the majority plays a significant role in this doctrine.

With Kelsen, the moderating device, associated with reviewing constitutionality, results from a particular understanding of the balance of powers that essentially grows out of respect for the constitution. The *'principle in which the balance of political forces is legally expressed'*[7] resides in the constitution. Accordingly, Kelsen attributes to a constitutional court the preservative power that guarantees the moderation of powers. The issue of the existence of a preservative or neutral power, as posed by Kelsen, is eminently topical. For example, in 2008 Patrice Rolland asked: 'is the idea of a power that preserves the institutions definitively unthinkable, at least in a democracy dealing with the sovereign will?'[8] Rolland gives the same answer to this question that Kelsen had given:

> Is the true guardian of the constitution not the judge, and especially the constitutional judge? Is not he the only true neutral power, in the sense that he does not constitute an 'active' power, and can be considered as independent of the other two?[9]

The constitutional court as a guarantor of constitutional liberties can be conducive to the moderation of majorities, an idea that figures prominently in current debates. Especially controversial is the compatibility of judicial review with the very principles of democracy. Among those who defend that compatibility, in addition to Hans Kelsen, are John Hart Ely[10] and Ronald Dworkin,[11] in opposition

---

7   H. Kelsen, 'La Garantie juridictionnelle de la Constitution', *La Revue du Droit Public et de la Science Politique en France et à l'Étranger*, 1928, vol. 45, p. 8 (emphasis added).

8   P. Rolland, 'Comment préserver les institutions politiques? La théorie du pouvoir neutre chez B. Constant', *Revue française d'histoire des idées politiques*, 2008, no. 27, p. 72.

9   ibid.

10   J. Hart Ely, *Democracy and Distrust: A Theory of Judicial Review*, Cambridge (MA): Harvard University Press, 1980.

11   R. Dworkin, *Taking Rights Seriously*, London: Duckworth, 2009.

to Jeremy Waldron[12] and Bruce Ackerman,[13] who look on judicial review as inconsistent with respecting democratic principles.

Political-Institutional Devices for Moderating Majority Decisions

It is often forgotten that in Kelsen's thinking, moderation of majority decisions also takes place through channels other than a constitutional court. For example, he examines political-institutional means to limit the negative impact of majority tyranny. Proportional voting systems are particularly important here, since they allow better representation of minority parties. According to Kelsen, the influence of minorities turns out to be so great that they are actually the most strongly represented, which is precisely what this type of election encourages:

> Proportional representation has or leads to an effect that we have recognised as the result of this interplay of forces that constitutes the essence of democratic party government. Here the will of the state is not determined by the interests of one group; rather, it is determined by a process in which the interests of various groups organised into parties struggle among themselves and reach a compromise. For the will of the state not to express the interest of just one party, there must be guarantees that as many party interests as possible can be expressed and enter into *competition*, so that eventually there will be a *compromise* among them.[14]

In Kelsen's view, compromise, as one of the means by which parliamentary regimes reduce the risk that majorities will abuse their power, plays a crucial role in democracies. As noted above, if there are no absolute values that can be proclaimed and imposed in democracies, the only way to overcome differences in a political community is for there to be compromises. These are the principal way of pacifying the representatives of opposing interests. Democracy being subject to permanent conflicts, a very well-tuned mechanism of compromise is essential to its survival. These reflections of Kelsen were particularly relevant in the climate of social divisions and class warfare that in the 1920s posed serious challenges to democratic thinking.

---

12 J. Waldron, 'The core of the case against judicial review', *The Yale Law Journal*, 2006, Vol. 115, pp. 1346–1406.

13 B. Ackerman, *We the People*, Cambridge (MA) and London: Harvard University Press, 1991.

14 H. Kelsen, *Vom Wesen und Wert der Demokratie*, Tübingen: J.C.B. Mohr, 1929, republished in H. Kelsen, *Verteidigung der Demokratie*, M. Jestaedt and O. Lepsius, (eds) Tübingen, Mohr Siebeck, 2006, p. 200 (original emphasis). It is also worth noting this other very illustrative statement: 'In proportional representation, ideally there are no losers, because no one is outvoted. To get elected, it is simply not necessary to receive a majority of votes, but only a "minimum", the calculation of which is precisely the distinctive feature of the art of proportional elections', ibid. p. 198.

In our day, comparative political science, notably the work of Arend Lijphart, has confirmed Kelsen's intuition: the 'consensus democracies' that are characterised by power sharing are more widely considered by their citizens to be 'kinder and gentler' regimes than are majoritarian democracies of the Westminster type, which are sometimes seen as elective dictatorships.[15]

Thus Kelsen expresses great confidence in the self-limiting capabilities of majorities. He sees the relationship between majorities and minorities, especially in parliamentary arenas, as being almost necessarily inclined towards compromise:

> A cursory glance at *parliamentary* practice is enough to see that the majority principle particularly in *parliamentary* systems turns out to be a principle of compromise, a balancing of political differences. In fact the whole of parliamentary procedure is addressed to reaching such a middle line between the opposing interests, a resultant of the antagonistic social forces. It creates guaranties that the various interests of groups represented in parliament are able to express themselves and to appear as such in a *public* process.[16]

The relationship between majority and minority, including compromises between them, has a prominent place in Kelsen's discussion of democracy. His conclusions raise some questions today: first, would the compromising that seems to him so necessary to the proper functioning of democracy, for pacifying the relationship between majority and minority, not be endangered by the revival of the imperative mandate that he so greatly aspired to? Second, are self-limitations by majorities, and therefore the practice of compromise, really as natural as all that in representative democracies? Third, are the arts of compromise really typical of democratic regimes? Fourth, if majority decision making is so naturally self-limiting, why do we have to think so much about ways to limit it?

First, Kelsen's support for the imperative mandate,[17] aimed at bringing the will of elected officials closer to that of the voters, seems to contradict his concept of democracy understood as a space for negotiation and compromise – among party leaders, for example. In fact, negotiation can occur only between agents who have some leeway with their principals, the people being represented, and this undermines the imperative mandate.[18]

---

15 A. Lijphart, *Patterns of Democracy: Government Forms and Performance in Thirty-Six Countries*, New Haven (CT), Yale University Press, 1999, p. 300.

16 H. Kelsen, *Vom Wesen und Wert der Demokratie*, (1929), republished in Hans Kelsen, *Verteidigung der Demokratie*, pp. 196–197 (original emphasis).

17 As we have seen in Chapter Two, the imperative mandate sees deputies in representative assemblies as agents or exponents of the interests of their electors rather than of the nation's interests.

18 As mentioned below, a concept of democracy as a space for negotiation is defended by Norberto Bobbio, among others.

Second, in Kelsen's account, the majority never seems to exclude the minority from the formation of the will of the state, out of fear of endangering the democratic process. So for him, the application of the principle of majority rule is accompanied almost naturally by a self-limitation. In the interwar period, Hermann Heller had already been less optimistic about this, when he emphasised the need to make sure that democracies contain integration mechanisms. Heller was thus suggesting that relations between majorities and minorities do not necessarily incline towards moderation, and can sink into violent power relations, for example if the minority has no realistic prospect of ever ending up in power, especially if its minority status includes structural characteristics linked to religion or language. In 1993 Fritz Scharpf, in 'Versuch über Demokratie im verhandelnden Staat' ('Essay on Democracy in the Negotiating State'), reformulated Heller's concerns when he recalled that the restrictions imposed by the majority on itself do not stand on their own, for they require conditions to which Kelsen perhaps paid too little attention. Indeed, accepting that the majority party (or coalition) will limit itself, for example by not imposing on the minority either unsustainable costs or norms that violate its identity, presupposes some degree of identification of the majority with the minority. To refer to the necessary identification of the different parts of the community with each other, Scharpf talks about a 'Wir-Identität' that makes it possible both for the majority not to abuse its power and for the minority not to feel the vote of the majority to which it is subject as an external domination, but rather as a mechanism for collective decision making. A deficit of 'Wir-Identität' would expose the minority to risks that Scharpf very clearly understood. When societies lack a feeling of sameness (Wir-Identität), mutual empathy and trust, there is a risk that majoritarian mechanisms will be used to pursue narrow utilitarian, individualistic or particularistic ends.[19]

Third, looking at compromise as a distinguishing feature of democratic life is also questioned in current research. In the light of studies of dictatorial regimes, is it really the case that they do not themselves regularly engage in compromise? For example, Jennifer Gandhi and Adam Przeworski question that idea, and note that dictatorships do resort to compromise, especially when confronted by a high risk of rebellion. If, in line with these writers, we admit that observation, then the Kelsenian characterisation of democracy – broadly associated with the idea of compromise – will be weakened:

---

19 See F. W. Scharpf, *Versuch über Demokratie im verhandelnden Staat*, in R. Czada and M. G. Schmidt (eds) *Verhandlungs-demokratie, Interessenvermittlung, Regierbarkeit*, Opladen: Westdeutscher Verlag, 1993, p. 26.

When the opposition is strong, the dictator makes more extensive policy compromises and shares some rents, just enough to prevent the opposition from rebelling. Finally, when the opposition has little chance of overthrowing the dictator but the dictator cannot inflict much damage on the opposition, the dictator offers few compromises and the opposition does rebel[20].

Of course, it could be argued that, while compromising may be necessary in autocracies when rebellion threatens, it is not the rule and is not even a natural response in such regimes, in contrast to democracies as understood by Kelsen (and others, for example Norberto Bobbio[21]).

Fourth, Kelsen seems remarkably contradictory when, on the one hand, he pays so much attention to political-legal devices for moderating majority decisions, while on the other, he displays excessive confidence in the majorities' self-restraint. I think this paradox can be explained partly by the discursive context from which these Kelsenian propositions emerged. Kelsen's optimism acted as a kind of counterweight to an intellectual climate that was suspicious about, or even hostile to, parliamentary systems. At the same time, his attempt to rescue the reputation of parliaments was not blind to their potential abuses, and therefore it recognised the need to constrain them, i.e. to moderate them.

The Accountability of Representatives

In addition to the issue of the limits that should be applied to self-government, another aspect of Kelsen's political thought strongly resonates in the current debates: the issue of the accountability of government, and voters' control over their representatives. Kelsen deals with this issue especially when he discusses the reform of parliamentary systems.[22] Some of the solutions that he proposed are timely today, while others now seem less relevant. Monitoring members of parliament is an issue that he tackles when he considers the imperative mandate and the need for publicity. The constitutional court, as already mentioned, is also a form of control.

In 1929, at a time when the need for publicity and the principle of transparency were not recognised nearly as much as they have been in recent years, Kelsen demonstrated that they are integral parts of democracy.[23] He did this by building

---

20 J. Gandhi and A. Przeworski, 'Cooperation, co-optation, and rebellion under dictatorships', *Economics and Politics*, 2006, vol. 18, p. 2.

21 See below, note 33.

22 Kelsen discusses this in his chapters on 'The reform of parliamentarianism' and 'The selection of leaders' in *Vom Wesen und Wert der Demokratie*.

23 This does not mean that there were no precursors to Kelsen on this subject. Since the end of the eighteenth century, writers such as Bentham, Kant, Rousseau and Constant had pointed out the

on the relativism that he had defended throughout his work. From the fact that a citizen who wins an election is not intrinsically superior to the voters, since the election result is not necessarily linked to the qualities of the winner, it follows that people who are elected must be subject to criticism. This critical spirit needs to be nourished by reliable information about the activities of elected officials, and this is supplied by publicity surrounding their deeds and their words. The accountability of governments becomes effective only through transparency:

> In the system of *democratic* ideology, the problem of creating leaders is at the centre of rational considerations, and leadership is definitely not an absolute but only a relative value. The leader is a 'leader' only for a certain period and in certain respects; he is otherwise an equal comrade and is subject to criticism. From this there also follows the *publicity* of government actions, in contrast to the principle of *confidentiality* in autocracies.[24]

In Kelsen's view, it is not just political accountability that depends on publicity; so does legality. In a democracy, the legality of the state's actions is best guaranteed by publicity.[25] In *The Structural Transformation of the Public Sphere*, Jürgen Habermas took up this argument in a very similar way: 'Just as secrecy was supposed to serve the maintenance of sovereignty based on *voluntas*, so publicity was supposed to serve the promotion of legislation based on *ratio*'.[26] While

---

importance of applying the principle of publicity to the pursuit of the common good; cf. S. Baume, 'La transparence dans la conduite des affaires publiques: sens et origines d'une exigence', *Raison Publique*, 11 July 2011, pp. 1–26, http://www.raison-publique.fr/article459.html, accessed on 21st June 2012.

24 H. Kelsen, *Vom Wesen und Wert der Demokratie*, pp. 216–217 (original emphasis). In Chapter One (page 14) we have seen the implications for democratic leadership that are conveyed by this passage.

25 'Since democracy is concerned with legal security, and thus with lawfulness and accountability in the workings of government, there is a strong inclination here to control-mechanisms, as a guarantee for the legality required. And the principle of publicity is therefore paramount, as the most effective guarantee. The tendency to disclosure is typically democratic, and tempts a superficial or ill-disposed judgement of this form of state to assume prematurely that certain political abuses, especially corruption, are commoner here than under autocracy, where in fact they merely remain invisible because the opposite system of government prevails. An absence of control-measures, which could only hamper the working of the state; no publicity, but an intensive effort, in the interests of state authority, to maintain it in awe, to reinforce official discipline and the obedience of the subject; in a word, concealment'. H. Kelsen, 'State-form and world-outlook', pp. 103–104.

26 J. Habermas, *The Structural Transformation of the Public Sphere: An inquiry into a category of bourgeois society*, trans. Thomas Burger (with the assistance of Frederick Lawrence), Cambridge (MA): MIT Press, 1991, p. 63. This work was first published in German in 1962, and first published

secrecy is an attribute of arbitrary power, publicity came to characterise legislators in the rational state. The justifications of publicity that were deployed by Kelsen, to defend applying the principle of transparency, are constantly expressed in the literature today. The legality of states' actions – the moralisation of the political – comes about especially through greater transparency in the management of public affairs.[27]

Revitalising the Imperative Mandate

Kelsen's support for the imperative mandate – as distinguished from the representative mandate – can be explained only by his consistent desire to strengthen the links between elected officials and their electorates. However, for him, this relationship is inconceivable without political parties acting as intermediaries. In his view, political parties are best able to aggregate and to represent voters. The understanding of the imperative mandate, in the second wind that Kelsen seeks to give to it, demands a very positive assessment of the role of parties, which he regards as the best representatives of civil society.

While the need for transparency, as called for by Kelsen in the 1920s, is very much in line with our outlook today, that is less true of the almost exclusive role that he gives to parties in representing civil society. Their place in democratic life now seems to be significantly modified and clearly weakened. Bernard Manin has very well described the passage from the 'party democracy' that emerged in the late nineteenth century and the 'audience democracy' that appeared in the last third of the twentieth century. While 'party democracy' gave parties a central role, making them highly structural in the lives of their members and in political life more generally, 'audience democracy' is characterised by a much looser relationship between political parties and citizens. Voters decide less and less often on the basis of traditional party loyalty and more and more on the basis of their current perceptions of what's politically on offer, perceptions which are conditioned by the media.[28] Electoral volatility generally characterises this second phase. Kelsen wrote most of his political reflections during the period of 'party democracy'. In *Party Government* (1942), E.E. Schattschneider captured the outlook on the role of political parties in democratic life which was shared by Kelsen when he published *Vom Wesen und Wert der Demokratie*:

---

in English in 1989.

27 C. Hood and D. Heald (eds), *Transparency: The key to better governance?*, Oxford: Oxford University Press, 2006.

28 Cf. B. Manin, *The Principles of Representative Government*, Cambridge: Cambridge University Press, 1997, pp. 193ff.

The rise of political parties is indubitably one of the principal distinguishing marks of modern government. The parties, in fact, have played a major role as makers of governments, more especially they have been the makers of democratic government. It should be stated flatly at the outset that this volume is devoted to the thesis that the political parties created democracy and that modern democracy is unthinkable save in terms of parties. As a matter of fact, the condition of the parties is the best possible evidence of the nature of any regime. The most important distinction in modern political philosophy, the distinction between democracy and dictatorship, can be made best in terms of party politics. The parties are not therefore merely appendages of modern government; they are in the centre of it and play a determinative and creative role in it.[29]

In contrast to the picture painted by Schattschneider, parties today are no longer the pivot of political life in democracies. They are no longer the exclusive carriers of the expressions of social preferences. As noted by Russell J. Dalton *et al.*, citizens can now influence decision making without going through a party, by forming public interest groups.[30] Consulting these groups plays a growing role in the development of legislation. 'Advocacy democracy' is the term often used to refer to the influence of lobbies and public interest groups. According to Peter Mair, the relative decline of political parties is also related to the fact that they are now discredited and distrusted, and this makes us doubt that they could serve as instruments for the revitalisation of democracy:

> Parties, like the other traditional institutions of the European polities, might well be considered by citizens as necessary for the good functioning of politics and the state, but they are neither liked nor trusted. Indeed, as is clear from the comparative survey evidence, parties are the least trusted of any of the major political institutions in contemporary democracy.[31]

However, it must be noted that the distrust of political parties that Mair emphasises especially in 'The Challenge to Party Government' was not something completely unfamiliar to Kelsen in the interwar period. Parliamentary government was then going through one of the largest crises it had ever known. For some writers – notably Carl Schmitt – political parties bore much of the blame for this.[32]

---

29 This citation was suggested to me by P. Mair, 'Democracy Beyond Parties' (2005), p.6–7, http://cadmus.eui.eu/bitstream/handle/1814/3291/viewcontent.pdf?sequence=1?./. Accessed 21st June 2012.

30 R. J. Dalton *et al.*, 'Democratic Publics and Democratic Institutions', in B. E. Cain *et al.*, *Democracy Transformed? Expanding political opportunities in advanced industrial democracies*, Oxford: Oxford University Press, 2003, p. 254.

31 P. Mair, 'The Challenge to Party Government', *West European Politics*, 2008, vol. 31, nos. 1–2, p. 230.

32 Cf. C. Schmitt, *The Crisis of Parliamentary Democracy*, trans. E. Kennedy, Cambridge Mass.:

Briefly surveying the current relevance of Kelsen's political thought shows that in several areas his thinking retains a vibrant topicality. First, consider the issue of limitations on majority decision making. Kelsen's support for that non-majoritarian institution, the constitutional court, as well as his marked preference for proportional voting systems, retain an obvious relevance to current debates. In addition, Kelsen's attention to the idea of compromise in democratic life is very topical. Norberto Bobbio was to be in perfect agreement with Kelsen on this, as noted by Adam Przeworski, here quoting Bobbio:

> The normal procedure for making decisions under democracy is one in which 'collective decisions are the fruit of negotiation and agreements between groups which represent social forces (unions) and political forces (parties) rather than an assembly where majority voting operates'.[33]

On the issue of government accountability, the role that Kelsen attributes to political parties in bringing together voters and elected officials is today probably the most doubtful item in the list, in great contrast to his views on transparency, which are being steadily revived in current discussions.

In the end, the lasting perceptiveness of Kelsen's reflections comes from the clarity with which he reasserts the basic principles of democracy, and from his lucidity about the dangers that can lurk in these principles. The topicality of Hans Kelsen's political thought resides especially in his correctives to these dangers, correctives that usually lead us in the direction of moderation.

MIT Press, 1988, pp. 20–21.

33 A. Prezworski, 'Self-Government in Our Times', quoting N. Bobbio, *The Future of Democracy*, Minneapolis: University of Minnesota Press, 1989, p. 116.

select bibliography of kelsen's writings

1905   Die Staatslehre des Dante Alighieri (*Dante Alighieri's Theory of the State*), Wiener staatswissenschaftliche Studien, vol. 6, Wien und Leipzig: Franz Deuticke, 1905, IV, 152 Seiten.

1911   *Hauptprobleme der Staatsrechtslehre: entwickelt aus der Lehre vom Rechtssatze* (*Principal Problems in the Theory of Public Law*),Tübingen: J.C.B. Mohr, 1923.

1911   *Über Grenzen zwischen juristischer und soziologischer Methode*, Tübingen: J.C.B. Mohr, 1911.

1913   'Politische Weltanschauung und Erziehung' in A. J. Merkl, and A. Verdross (eds), *Die Wiener Rechtstheoretische Schule*, Wien: Europa Verlag, 1968, pp. 1501–1524.

1920   *Vom Wesen und Wert der Demokratie*, Tübingen, J.C.B. Mohr, 1920.

1920   *Das Problem der Souveränität und die Theorie des Völkerrechts Beitrag zu einer reinen Rechtslehre*, Tübingen, J.C.B. Mohr, 1920.

1921   'Demokratisierung der Verwaltung' in A. J. Merkl, and A. Verdross (eds), *Die Wiener Rechtstheoretische Schule*, Wien: Europa Verlag, 1968, pp. 1581–1591.

1922   'Der Begriff des Staates und die Sozialpsychologie: Mit besonderer Berücksichtigung von Freuds Theorie der Masse', *Imago*, vol. 8, 1922, pp. 97–141.

1922   *Der soziologische und der juristische Staatsbegriff: Kritische Untersuchung des Verhältnisses zwischen Staat und Recht*, Aalen: Scientia Verlag, 1962.

1922–23 'Gott und Staat', *Logos*, Internationale Zeitschrift für Philosophie der Kultur, vol. 11, 1922–1923, pp. 261- 284.
'God and the State', in O. Weinberger (ed. and intro.), *Hans Kelsen: Essays in Legal and Moral Philosophy*, trans. P. Heath, Dordrecht (Netherlands) and Boston (USA): D. Reidel Publishing Company, 1973, pp. 61–82.

1923   'Die politische Theorie des Sozialismus', Österreichische Rundschau, 19th Jahrgang, 1923, pp. 113–135.

1923   *Sozialismus und Staat: Eine Untersuchung der politischen Theorie des Marxismus*, Leipzig: C. L. Hirschfeld, 1923.

1924   'The conception of the state and social psychology: with special reference to Freud's group theory', *International Journal of Psycho-Analysis*, 1924, vol. 5, pp. 1–38.

1925   *Allgemeine Staatslehre*, Berlin: Julius Springer, 1925.

1925   *Das Problem des Parlamentarismus*, Wien: Leipzig, Wilhelm Braumüller, 1925.

1925   *Introduction to the Problems of Legal Theory: A Translation of the First Edition of the Reine Rechtslehre or Pure Theory of Law*, trans. B. Litschewski Paulson and S. L. Paulson, Intro. S. L. Paulson, Oxford: Clarendon Press, 1992.

1926   'Aperçu d'une théorie générale de l'État', *Revue du Droit public et de la science politique*, 1926, no. 4, pp. 561–646.

1926   *Der Staat als Übermensch*, Wien: Springer, 1926.

1927   'Demokratie', in A. J. Merkl and A. Verdross (eds), *Die Wiener Rechtstheoretische Schule*, Wien: Europa Verlag, 1968, pp. 1743–1776.

1927   'Selsbstdarstellung' in M. Jestaedt (ed.), *Hans Kelsen im Selbstzeugnis*, Tübingen: Mohr Siebeck, 2006, pp. 21–29.

1928 'La Garantie juridictionnelle de la Constitution', *La Revue du Droit public et de la Science politique en France et à l'Étranger*, 1928, vol. 45, pp. 1–61.

1928 'Wesen und Entwicklung der Staatsgerichtsbarkeit', in H. Triepel, M. Layer, and E. von Hippel (eds), *Verhandlungen der Tagung der Deutschen Staatsrechtslehrer zu Wien am 23 und 24 April 1928* (*Negotiations of the Conference on German Constitutional Law at Vienna on 23 and 24 April 1928*), 1929, pp. 30–84.

1928–32 *Der Staat als Integration: Eine prinzipielle Auseinandersetzung*, Aalen: Scientia Verlag, 1971.

1929 *Vom Wesen und Wert der Demokratie*, Tübingen: J.C.B. Mohr, 1929. Republished in *Verteidigung der Demokratie*, M. Jestaedt and O. Lepsius (eds), Tübingen: Mohr Siebeck, 2006, pp. 149–228.

1929 'Geschworengericht und Demokratie: Das Prinzip der Legalität', in A. J. Merkl and A. Verdross (eds), *Die Wiener Rechtstheoretische Schule*, Wien: Europa Verlag, 1968, pp. 1777–1779.

1931 *Der Wandel des Souveränitätsbegriffes* (excerpt from *Studi filosofico-giuridici dedicati a Giorgio del Vecchio*), Modena: Società tipografica modenese, 1931.

1931 *Wer soll der Hüter der Verfassung sein?*, (*Who Should Be the Guardian of the Constitution?*), Berlin: W. Rothschild, 1931.
Qui doit être le gardien de la Constitution?, Paris, Michel Houdiard, 2006.

1933 'Lettre à Renato Treves', *Droit et société*, 1987, no. 7, pp. 326–329.

1933 *Recht und Staat in Geschichte und Gegenwart*, Tübingen: J.C.B. Mohr, 1933.

1933 'State-Form and World-Outlook', in O. Weinberger (ed. and intro.), *Hans Kelsen: Essays in Legal and Moral Philosophy*, trans. P. Heath, Dordrecht (Netherlands) and Boston (USA): D. Reidel Publishing Company, 1973, pp. 95–113.

1934 *La dictature de parti*, Paris: Institut international de droit public, 1934.

1934 'La Méthode et la notion fondamentale de la théorie pure du droit', *Revue de Métaphysique et de Morale*, 1934, pp. 183–204.

1934 *Reine Rechtslehre* (*Pure Theory of Law*) Vienna: F. Deuticko.

1936 'The Party-Dictatorship', *Politica*, vol. 2, 1936, pp. 19–32

1937 'The Function of the Pure Theory of Law', in A. Reppy (ed.), *Law: A Century of Progress 1835–1935*, 3 vols., New York: New York University Press and London: Oxford University Press, 1937, vol. 2, pp. 231–241.

1945 *General Theory of Law and State*, trans. A. Wedberg, Cambridge, Mass.: Harvard University Press, 1945. Reprinted in Clark, New Jersey: The Lawbook Exchange, Ltd., 2011.

1948 'Absolutism and Relativism in Philosophy and Politics', *The American Political Science Review*, vol. 2, 1948, pp. 906–914.

1948 *The Political Theory of Bolshevism: A critical analysis*, Berkeley: University of California Press.

1950 *The Law of the United Nations: A critical analysis of its fundamental problems*, Published under the auspices of the London Institute of World Affairs, London: Stevens & Sons; New York: Frederick A. Praeger Inc. 1950.

1952 *Principles of International Law*, New York: Rinehart & Co, 1952.

1955 'Foundations of Democracy', *Ethics*, 1955, vol. 66, no. 1, pp. 1–101.

1957 *Collective Security under International Law*, Naval War College, Newport, Rhode Island. International Law Studies. 1954 (1956); *Navpers* 15031, Volume XLIX, Washington: United States Government Printing Office, 1957.

1982 *Il Primato del Parlamento*, Milan: Giuffré.

index

A

'Absolutism and Relativism in Philosophy and Politics' xv
accountability, political 51, 57, 58, 61
Ackerman, B. 54
'advocacy democracy' 60
Allgemeine Staatslehre 10, 11, 25, 26, 29, 33, 44–5
anarchism 9
Anschütz, G. 11, 28 n.32, 38
Association of German Law Teachers 27–8
Austria xiv, 1, 3
  Christian Social Party (CSP) 3
  Constitution (1920) 38
  Constitutional Court 3, 34
    matrimonial waiver (1929) 3, 34
  constitutional reform in 2, 3, 23, 37
    model of constitutional law 38
  republic, formation of xiv
  Social Democratic Party (SDP) 3
Austrian Journal of Public Law 2
authoritarianism 31
autocracy 10, 13, 14, 15, 19, 21, 25, 51
  democracy and 13, 14, 19, 20, 29, 51, 52, 57
  dynamic/static integration and 29
  political leaders and 14, 58
  political stability in 30
autonomy, principle of 19, 21
  majority rule and 22
  parties, political and 23
  representative democracy and 24, 51, 52

B

Barthélemy, J. xii
Baume, S. xv, 25 n.24, 58 n.23
Beaud, O. xvi n.26
Béguin, J.-C. 38 n.74
Bentham, J. 57 n.23
Bernatzik, E. 2
Bobbio, N. 7, 8 n.6, 55 n.18, 57, 61
bolshevism 9, 10, 24
Bonn, M. J. 25, 28
Borgeaud, C. 25
Boudon, R. 9 n.8
Brunner, E. 12, 15
Burke, E. 32

C

Cain, B. E. 60 n.30
Caldwell, P. C. xiv n.17
Calsamiglia, A. xiii
capitalism 9
  democracy and xiv, 16–17, 18 n.38
Carrino, A. xv
Catholicism 9
  marriage indissolubility 3–4, 34
  Pope, infallibility of 47, 49
Chagnollaud, D. 37 n.71
church-state relations 34
civil society 23, 24, 31
class warfare 30–1, 54
Collective Security under International Law 4
communism 9
compromise, principle of 29–31, 54–6, 61
  definition of 29–30
  dictatorships and 56
  minorities/majorities 29–30, 54–6

Lightning Source UK Ltd.
Milton Keynes UK
UKOW040114220213

206651UK00002B/13/P